ANCHORED IN CHRIST:

Daily Devotionals from Philippians

ERIC E. PRATT, Ph.D.

Published by:

The Carpenter's Table Publishing

www.AtTheTableWithHim.com

ISBN (Paperback): 979-8-9940497-0-9

ISBN (eBook): 979-8-9940497-2-3

ISBN (Hardcover): 979-8-9940497-1-6

Library of Congress Control Number:

Printed in the United States of America

First Edition: 2026

Cover design & illustration:

Interior layout:

There are three things that I believe make Anchored in Christ a very special devotional. First, the source material is the book of Philippians and there's no more encouraging, instructive, and anointed book in the New Testament than this one. Second, the insights and wisdom that Dr. Pratt brings to the attention of the reader are more than helpful. They come from lived experience, decades of ministry and service, and walking with Christ as both his Savior and friend. And finally, I just love Eric Pratt. Simply put, he is one of the best and most godly men I have known in my life and I trust the way he handles God's word.

> **Clayton King,** Pastor, Evangelist, Author Crossroads Camps & Conferences & Minister in Residence, Anderson University

I have read, reflected, repented, and renewed my relationship with Christ through Dr. Pratt's daily devotionals for more than a decade. These writings have consistently challenged me to go deeper with the Lord even when it cost me more. They have convicted me when I was wrong and encouraged me to stand firm when I was right, even in the face of opposition. In seasons of struggle, storms, and sadness, I have found both comfort and confidence through these reflections.

"Anchored in Christ" is written with the heart of a shepherd, the faithfulness of a friend, and the dedication of a true disciple. I wholeheartedly endorse Anchored in Christ: Daily Devotionals from Philippians not only because of the revelation and insight it offers, but because of the sincere, Christ-centered heart of the author who writes them.

> **Neddie Winters,** Former President
> Mission Mississippi

Thirty years ago, a professor at one of our Baptist seminaries walked up to me at Ridgecrest Baptist Assembly and urged me to speak to my husband about employing Dr. Eric Pratt as campus minister at the college where Lee was then president. I was at Ridgecrest teaching with some of my dear colleagues from my former career as an editor at LifeWay Christian Resources.

When the Pratts came to interview, we began a long journey together in Christian ministry, working together for the Lord at two universities over 23 years. That day, I met his special wife Penny and his son Paul, then a toddler. Over all those years, I have seen Eric and

Penny live out their Christian commitment in unselfish, unflagging, and unusual ways in good times in their lives and in deeply challenging ones. Eric is creative, busy, and always motivating others to service.

For a number of years, Eric has been blessing those of us on his email list with his daily devotions, usually sent at times such as 4:30 a.m. He has refined his skills to a high level of writing and Christian scriptural explication. Each day's devotional gives me something to remember, think about, and do. I recommend this blessing to anyone who wants to learn from a thorough, faithful, tried and true Christian servant.

Rhoda Royce, Former Editor
Open Windows

Eric's writings are Holy Spirit filled with insightful wisdom that is applicable to everyday life. You will grow deeper in your love for Jesus reading his devotionals on a daily basis.

Mike MacIntyre, Football Coach
2016 NCAA Coach of the Year

Dr. Pratt brings a genuine and personal touch to his understanding of Scripture and to what it means to live in joy on a daily basis. I had the privilege of working with him for more than a dozen years. He writes what he believes and lives what he writes. May you find joy in the reading of his devotionals.

Dr. Wayne VanHorn, Professor of Christian Studies
Mississippi Christian University

In need of a daily reminder that the Creator of the universe cares for you? Dr. Pratt offers an inspiring commentary on daily scripture designed to uplift you, deepen your relationship with God, and provide wisdom and insights as you seek to grow in your faith. Through *Anchored in Christ: Daily Devotionals from Philippians*, Dr. Pratt guides readers through Paul's letter to the Philippians, offering profound commentary, reflective questions, and heartfelt prayers.

I eagerly anticipate each day's devotion, as it serves as a stabilizing force for my day.

Deborah Davis, Ed.D
Found of Kinship C&C

I met Eric a few years ago when he and his wife Penny walked into our Bible study class at church. We exchanged the usual greetings then took our seats. As our teacher was presenting the lesson, I glanced over at Eric and saw him writing in his notebook. Profusely. I had only known him for five minutes but knew instantly he was a kindred spirit. He shares my love of the Bible and of writing.

From there it didn't take long for our cadre of teachers to lure him into the rotation. I have learned much from his insights on the scriptures. There is one thing I can always tell after listening to one of his lessons. I can see how much time he has spent with Jesus. Not just how much time he spent preparing the lesson.

I trust you will find the same when reading these devotionals. Eric writes out of a love for the Lord first. What flows from that is wisdom and practical insight. And what I find refreshing in his writing is that he doesn't write merely to make you feel good. He writes to push you closer to Jesus.

These short devotionals give you a passage of scripture and a practical way to apply it to your life. And he ends each with a heartfelt prayer that is a great guide if you struggle in this spiritual discipline. I invite you to spend ten minutes of your time in God's word, Eric's insight and prayer. I can't think of a better way to begin your day.

Dave Dingess, Author & Consultant

Anchored in Christ by Dr. Eric Pratt spiritually and skillfully leads us through the book that Paul wrote to the Church in Philippi. He encourages us through daily devotions to be rooted and grounded in our relationship with Christ. Life has a way of greeting us with a never-ending supply of challenges. Philippians gives us encouragement, direction, and even instructs our attitude when the inevitable difficulties of life come our way.

Absorb this book. Allow God to do a work of grace in you as you read it. It is a journey worthy of your time, investment, and devotion.

David Leavell, Ph.D., Pastor
Faceville Baptist Church

Eric makes the Bible approachable, inviting readers into its pages with clarity and grace. By providing context about each scripture's author and the challenges they were addressing, he deepens understanding and illuminates meaning. Through his thoughtful use of questions, he helps readers recognize how these ancient words still speak powerfully into their own lives today. What shines through most is Eric's humility: the reader can sense his genuine desire to grow in faith right alongside them, making the journey one of shared discovery rather than instruction alone.

Kelly Addeo, Executive Director
RISE UP!

Time spent in the book of Philippians is always worth it. Eric helps the reader slow down and think about all that God might be saying through this wonderful book with this devotional. All who take the time to work through this devotional will benefit from it.

Dr. Norris Grubbs, Provost
Professor of New Testament and Greek
New Orleans Baptist Theological Seminary

Eric is a gifted writer that pours out godly insights and encouragement that are simple, yet profound. He has a way with words. His devotions are so often just what I need to hear - focused on God's Word and counsel. His writing is full of golden nuggets of encouragement from God's treasure, His Word. I highly recommend this daily devotional on Philippians. It will inspire, challenge (in a good way), and uplift you.

Amy Conrod, Georgia State Coordinator
Moms in Prayer International

One of Eric's great assets is his smile. It is the type of smile that shows up in his eyes too. It is genuine. It has been great to teach with him in our Bible study class at our church. When he teaches he not only treats the text with accuracy but also with special insights that help explain the context, history and importance of what we are studying. He often has thought provoking questions that help me apply the passage to my life. Eric is also a person of prayer. He regularly follows up on prayer requests and sends encouraging texts. I believe that as you spend time in these devotional thoughts you will see Eric insights and sense his care. And if you are really paying attention you will be able to imagine him smiling warmly at you as you spend time with God.

Walter Shaffer, Missionary with Cru

Over the past several years, I have been extremely blessed in reading and applying Dr. Pratt's weekly devotionals in my daily prayer times. His family and mine have been connected for over 30 years as friends and fellow believers, so this makes his words ring even more special during this time of life. I know they will be just as encouraging to you and your family. May Christ bless you all as I recommend this read without hesitation.

Dr. Billy Moss, Pastor
Rockdale Baptist Church

Dr. Eric Pratt has been a dear friend of mine for more than 15 years. He has always shown himself to be a brother in the Lord and shares the utmost love for God. He has personally been a spiritual guide for me in my life. He has always provided good words of spiritual encouragement using the word of God. I am certain this book will provide enrichment to each and every person looking to walk closer with God, one day at a time, in daily devotional time.

Johnny Donaldson, Chief Culture Officer
BankPlus, Jackson, MS

Contents

Acknowledgements

This devotional journey would not have taken shape without the encouragement, support, and love of many.

To Penny, my greatest encourager and wisest counselor, thank you for nudging me to put these devotionals into a book. Your belief in the value of these reflections gave me the courage to share them more broadly.

To Daniel Memorial Baptist Church, thank you for being my guinea pig, the first congregation to walk through these thoughts with me, offering both insight and grace along the way.

To my small group and co-workers, your steady encouragement, thoughtful feedback, and genuine interest have meant more to me than you know. Thank you for spurring me on.

To my old friends (Mike, Gary, Clayton, Brian, Joey, Jeff, Dwayne, Lewis, Daryl, Bill, Tray, John, Paul, Johnny, and Neddie), because as we all know, we can never make new old friends, thank you for always believing I might have something worth saying. Your loyalty is a gift.

To Dr. Lee and Rhoda Royce, your continued encouragement and support have bolstered my faith and given me the confidence to push out my devotionals to a wider audience.

To my kids, Grace, Paul, and Chip, your presence in my life gives depth to everything I write. Watching you grow has sharpened my faith and deepened my understanding of grace.

And finally, to my Mom, thank you for always listening without judgment. You believed in me and my abilities before anyone else.

This book is for all of you.

Foreward

The letter of the Apostle Paul to the Philippians may be my favorite book of the Bible. I have taught and preached from these extraordinary texts of scripture. Some of its verses I have committed to memory, recalling them to mind in times of fear, anxiety, trial, and in almost every other condition in life. I stand amazed that Paul could radiate such wisdom, love, faith, and confident joy while chained to a Roman guard in a dark, fetid prison cell. I remain hopeful that I too might walk with some of Paul's confident faith and joy when life's trials close in on me.

As you experience these daily readings, enjoy the sharp, insightful, and powerful manner in which Dr. Eric Pratt brings Paul's inspired teachings to life, always pointing the reader toward spiritual maturity in Christ. Dr. Pratt brings decades of experience as a minister, chaplain, teacher at the undergraduate and seminary level, and university and school administrator to the daunting task of interpreting and applying some of the most profound truths of the Christian life. Dr. Pratt's professional career and the challenges he faced have prepared him well in presenting an exceptional devotional study of an extraordinary and powerful sacred letter.

When I first read these devotionals, I made notes in a journal for future reference, and I think you may do the same. Let these devotionals draw you closer to Christ, which of course is the intention of the Apostle Paul and of the devotional writer. May God bless you in this journey.

Lee Royce, President Emeritus
Mississippi College

Preface

Dr. Eric Pratt has been a friend since I was a professor, and he was a PhD student. I will spare you the math. In all those years, Dr. Pratt has served in a number of settings, in various roles and with several senior leaders. He has served in collegiate, denomination, convention, association, church, and private school settings. This book (as I read it), represents his heart to serve regardless of role. As you read *Anchored in Christ: Daily Devotionals from Philippians,* you will become quickly aware that Eric can write daily devotionals because he has personal devotion time with God daily. He often texts me (and I assume many others) with personal individualized prayers that flow out of his early morning time.

Anchored in Christ describes both Eric's teaching and his practice. I am intrigued with the opening lines in which Dr. Pratt confesses that he struggled with the reality that God still communicates personally, and sometimes audibly to those who seek Him. As a PhD student, Eric was intensely diligent, analytical, and attentive to the "finer points" of an assignment. I can understand how he would question that God would violate rational and expected norms to whisper audibly to a person who was seeking to understand the way of Jesus. The potential reader of this devotional will identify with the confession on the second paragraph of the introduction: "...I began to take time to listen. And in making space for God to speak, my life slowly changed being transformed by a consistent, internal conversation with my heavenly Father. Scripture makes it clear that God loves to talk with His children." It is the only devotional book I have ever read with an appendix to make sure that we understand the context as we consider what God says to us through the words of scripture.

Philippians is a personal letter from Paul to a church whom he intensely loved. Dr. Pratt masterfully takes an intimate, personal letter to a church and lets it become an intensely personal letter to a follower of Jesus who would spend three months in daily reading and contemplation. Eric tells us where he is going over 105 days, we will visit major themes of Philippians which are also major action points in daily discipleship. Among them are rejoicing in the Lord regardless of circumstances, growing in love and unity as the body of Christ, following Christ's example of humility and service, guarding against false teaching and misplaced confidence, pressing on toward maturity in Christ, and resting in the peace of God through prayer.

Before you read Day 1, you know that the words you read will be both ancient and contemporary, both academic and practical, and both well-researched and well-experienced by the author. You will know that the church at Philippi was much like our churches today with good days and bad days, good leadership decisions and questionable ones, and full of disciples of all genders, ages, and backgrounds. And so, the book flows, challenging us to open our hearts to whatever amazing and unprecedented thing God wants to do, through the great Christ hymn of Philippians 2:9-11, to the life instructions in chapter 4 verse 8 (which Dr. Pratt leads us through for an entire week!).

Eric describes the life lived according to Paul's instructions to this beloved church as "Father-filtered faith." He advocates a faith that "keeps coming back to grace" and Eric is so committed to God's wonderful gift of grace that he named his daughter after it. Life has not been easy for Eric, and I suspect for many of the readers of this incredible devotion. However, we are challenged to thank God for closed doors that became new directions, for hardships that shape our hearts, and for the people who come alongside in the journey. I am grateful for a book that is designed to walk a few steps with a reader on their journey to a faith that is filtered by words that the Father speaks personally, and sometimes audibly.

Dr. R. Allen Jackson
Atlanta, Georgia

Introduction

For much of my Christian life, I believed God didn't like to talk to me. My experience led me to think that God only spoke a few times audibly in history and only to people like Moses, David, or Paul, but never to a regular person like me. Then one day, I clearly heard God speak. I asked Him a question out of desperation, and He spoke. The Creator of the universe broke through the walls of my misconceptions and spoke to my heart in a voice so clearly it couldn't be mistaken.

After this happened, I began to take time to listen. And in making space for God to speak, my life slowly changed, being transformed by a consistent, internal conversation with my heavenly Father. Scripture makes it clear that God loves to talk with His children.

Whoever is of God hears the words of God.
John 8:47

Call to me and I will answer you, and will tell you great and hidden things that you have not known.
Jeremiah 33:3

*Incline your ear, and come to me;
hear, that your soul may live.*
Isaiah 55:3

*I will instruct you and teach you in the way you should go;
I will counsel you with my eye upon you.*
Psalm 32:8

The list of Scriptures goes on and on. In story after story, the people of God hear God and know His will. The Bible is clear that God speaks to all of us as His children in a way we can understand through any and every means possible.

God speaks through all sorts of avenues. Most assuredly, He speaks to us through His Word. The Bible is one of our greatest gifts as Christians. It is the very word of God, *"...living and active, sharper than any two-edged sword, piercing to the division of soul and of spirit, of joints and of marrow, and discerning the thoughts and intentions of the heart"* (**Hebrews 4:12**).

God also speaks directly to us through His Holy Spirit. **John 16:13** says, *"When the Spirit of truth comes, he will guide you into all the truth, for he will not speak on his own authority, but whatever he hears he will speak, and he will declare to you the things that are to come."* And Scripture reveals how God speaks through His creation. **Romans 1:20** says that God's *"invisible attributes, namely, his eternal power and divine nature, have been clearly perceived, ever since the creation of the world, in the things that have been made."*

God loves to speak. He is not silent. He is not distant. He longs for us to live with the knowledge of His love and perfect will. The question is not whether God speaks. The question is, will we listen? Will we choose to submit ourselves to Him to receive and then obey what He would tell us? The first time God spoke directly to me, He asked me to do something incredibly difficult. It did not make total sense. But I knew He spoke. And in submission, I obeyed His command, and my life has been different ever since.

Listen to God today. Quiet your soul and receive the gift of conversation with your heavenly Father. God has placed His Spirit within you, closer to you than you can fully comprehend. You are unified with God. Ask the Spirit to reveal to you God's Word today. Ask God to make you aware of any and every avenue He desires to speak through. Then listen with an obedient, receptive heart to all the wonderful things He longs to tell you.

BACKGROUND About the Book of Philippians

In 2015, I did something simple, almost accidental, that God would later use in ways I never expected. I began gathering pieces of my journal, the quiet scribbles and prayers that had been shaping my walk with Christ, and I turned them into short devotionals I shared with my church members, a few friends, and family members. Nothing polished. Nothing strategic. Just honest reflections on Scripture and the Christian life.

What started as a handful of emails slowly began to grow. Someone would reply asking if they could forward a devotional to a friend. A former church member reached out to request being added. A coworker asked if their spouse could also receive them. Before long, my once-occasional notes evolved into weekly devotionals, and those weekly notes, prompted by God and encouraged by people, eventually became daily emails sent to anyone who requested to be included.

The pages that follow are drawn from those years of writing, praying, wrestling, and reflecting. They are devotional snapshots, verse by verse, day by day, walking through the book of Philippians. These devotionals were written for real people facing real joys, real struggles, and real questions. People I love. People trying to follow Jesus in the everyday, ordinary aspects of life.

I invite you to spend a few minutes with the Lord each day reflecting on the joy, encouragement, and instruction given to the church in Philippi. Paul wrote this letter from prison, yet his words ring with hope, gratitude, and confidence in Christ.

He encouraged the Philippians to keep their eyes fixed on Jesus, to rejoice in the Lord, and to live in unity and humility. The same encouragement is for us today. If we fix our eyes on Christ, cultivate joy in Him, and serve others in love, our lives will shine with the gospel.

Paul was a man who knew suffering, but he also knew joy that transcends circumstances. Chained to Roman guards, uncertain of his future, he still rejoiced. His joy was not rooted in freedom, comfort, or success; it was anchored in Christ. That is why this letter speaks so powerfully: it shows us how to live joyfully, humbly, and courageously in any season of life.

The church in Philippi was dear to Paul. It was the first church he planted in Europe, and its members were his faithful partners in the gospel. Paul's letter to them is deeply personal, filled with affection, prayer, and exhortation. He points them to Christ's example of humility, warns them against false teachers, and encourages them to press on toward the prize of knowing Christ fully.

Over the course of this short letter, Paul highlights key themes that help Christ followers live faithfully:

- Rejoicing in the Lord regardless of circumstances

- Growing in love and unity as the body of Christ

- Following Christ's example of humility and service

- Guarding against false teaching and misplaced confidence

- Pressing on toward maturity in Christ, and

- Resting in the peace of God through prayer.

Paul concludes with a note of gratitude, thanking the Philippians for their partnership and generosity. This letter overflows with joy, hope, and encouragement. As we study Philippians, may we discover the same joy Paul found in Christ, a joy that cannot be shaken by hardship, but instead shines as a testimony to the watching world.

My prayer is that as you read, you will hear the heartbeat of Paul's letter: joy rooted not in circumstances, but in Christ Himself. May these devotionals invite you to slow down, breathe deep, and sit with the One who began a good work in you, and who promises to carry it all the way to completion.

Welcome to the journey through Philippians. I am grateful you are here.

Ready to Learn, Live, and Love,

Colossians 2:2-3

DAY 1
The Church in Philippi

Paul came also to Derbe and to Lystra. A disciple was there, named Timothy, the son of a Jewish woman who was a believer, but his father was a Greek. The brothers at Lystra and Iconium well spoke of him. Paul wanted Timothy to accompany him, and he took him and circumcised him because of the Jews who were in those places, for they all knew that his father was a Greek. As they went on their way through the cities, they delivered to them for observance the decisions that had been reached by the apostles and elders who were in Jerusalem. So the churches were strengthened in the faith, and they increased in numbers daily.

And they went through the region of Phrygia and Galatia, having been forbidden by the Holy Spirit to speak the word in Asia. And when they had come up to Mysia, they attempted to go into Bithynia, but the Spirit of Jesus did not allow them. So, passing by Mysia, they went down to Troas. And a vision appeared to Paul in the night: a man of Macedonia was standing there, urging him and saying, "Come over to Macedonia and help us." And when Paul had seen the vision, immediately we sought to go on into Macedonia, concluding that God had called us to preach the gospel to them.

So, setting sail from Troas, we made a direct voyage to Samothrace, and the following day to Neapolis, and from there to Philippi, which is a leading city of the district of

Macedonia and a Roman colony. We remained in this city some days.
Acts 16:1-12

Have you ever felt like your good, godly plans were met with a closed door? That is precisely what Paul, Silas, and Timothy experienced in **Acts 16.** They were determined to preach the gospel to as many people as possible. Yet twice in this passage, the Holy Spirit blocked their path (**v.6–7**) not because their mission was wrong, but because God had something better in mind.

We often think the path should be clear if our intentions are pure. But that is not always the case. God's "No" is sometimes the road to a better "Yes." His guidance does not always come through green lights and smooth paths; it often shows up in the detours.

Paul's team did not throw in the towel. They continued to move forward, trusting God to lead them. Then, in a vision, Paul saw a man from Macedonia pleading for help (**v.9**). That vision became the turning point. They set sail immediately, confident that God's call had finally come into focus.

The result? The gospel took root in Europe, as evidenced by Lydia's conversion, the Philippian jailer's salvation, and the birth of the church at Philippi. It all started with two closed doors and one God-given vision.

When our plans are blocked, do not assume they are doomed to failure. They may be **Father-Filtered**. Our job is to stay faithful, keep walking, and trust that the God who directs our steps sees the bigger picture. Like Paul, be willing to pivot. Like Timothy, be willing to go. Like Silas, be willing to trust.

And remember, even the closed doors are still under God's control.

Father, thank You for guiding us even when we don't understand. Help us trust You when the road shifts or the doors shut. Give us willing hearts like Paul's, ready to follow wherever You lead. Open our eyes to the bigger picture You are painting, and give us joy in the journey, even when it takes unexpected turns.

God's guidance does not always come through green lights and smooth paths; it often shows up in the detours.

DAY 2
Letting the Lord Lead

And on the Sabbath day we went outside the gate to the riverside, where we supposed there was a place of prayer, and we sat down and spoke to the women who had come together. One who heard us was a woman named Lydia, from the city of Thyatira, a seller of purple goods, who was a worshiper of God. The Lord opened her heart to pay attention to what was said by Paul. And after she was baptized, and her household as well, she urged us, saying, "If you have judged me to be faithful to the Lord, come to my house and stay." And she prevailed upon us.
Acts 16:13-15

It was not a cathedral. Not even a chapel. Just a riverbank and a few women gathered in prayer: no pulpit, no organ, no stained glass. But heaven was leaning in.

In the quiet swirl of conversation, Scripture says, "*The Lord opened her heart.*" Lydia was not just any woman. She was a business owner. Sharp. Independent. She sold purple cloth to the upper class. She had success, but something was missing. Paul opened his mouth that day by the water, but God opened her heart.

Isn't that how God still works?

Maybe there is someone in your life you have been praying for. You have said the right things and shared your heart, but still, nothing has changed. It is not our power or attempts that bring someone to Jesus; it is His. He is still in the business of opening hearts.

Lydia did not just believe. She responded. She opened her home. She became a foundational part of the Philippian church; the very group Paul would later call his "*joy and crown.*"

Be faithful to speak, but trust God to work. Be ready to share, but let Him do the opening.

Lord, we surrender the hearts we care about to You. Thank You for opening ours. Help us to be faithful like Paul and responsive like Lydia.

DAY 3
God is Present

As we were going to the place of prayer, we were met by a slave girl who had a spirit of divination and brought her owners much gain by fortune-telling. She followed Paul and us, crying out, "These men are servants of the Most High God, who proclaim to you the way of salvation." And this she kept doing for many days. Paul, having become greatly annoyed, turned and said to the spirit, "I command you in the name of Jesus Christ to come out of her." And it came out that very hour.

But when her owners saw that their hope of gain was gone, they seized Paul and Silas and dragged them into the marketplace before the rulers. And when they had brought them to the magistrates, they said, "These men are Jews, and they are disturbing our city. They advocate customs that are not lawful for us as Romans to accept or practice." The crowd joined in attacking them, and the magistrates tore the garments off them and gave orders to beat them with rods. And when they had inflicted many blows upon them, they threw them into prison, ordering the jailer to keep them safely. Having received this order, he put them into the inner prison and fastened their feet in the stocks.
Acts 16:16–24

Sometimes, doing the right thing leads to painful consequences. That is what Paul and Silas experienced in Philippi. They were not picking a fight or breaking the law. They set a slave girl free from spiritual bondage. But that act of compassion unraveled her owners' profits, and suddenly, a crowd rose in outrage.

Beaten. Stripped. Imprisoned. Chained. All for doing what was good and godly.

It does not feel right or fair, does it?

Obedience to God does not always lead to applause. Sometimes it leads to pain. But Paul and Silas knew that faithfulness in the fire matters as much as fruitfulness on the mountaintop.

They did not rage against injustice or question God's goodness. Instead, in the very next verse, we find them praying and singing hymns to God in a prison cell (**v.25**). Why? Because they knew something we often forget: God is just as present in prison as He is in the pulpit.

Suppose we are walking through a season where obedience has cost us our comfort, reputation, and stability. Take heart: God wastes nothing. Even our pain has a purpose.

The same prison that held Paul and Silas became the stage for a miracle. A jailer's life would be changed, a household would find salvation, and the church in Philippi would gain a story of courage that would echo through eternity.

Lord, give us the courage to obey You even when it costs us. When we are misunderstood, misjudged, or mistreated, remind us that You see, care, and are with us. Help us sing through the suffering, trusting that Your plans are still unfolding in the dark places. Use our trials for Your glory.

*Obedience to God does not always lead to applause.
Sometimes it leads to pain.*

DAY 4
A Song in the Night

About midnight Paul and Silas were praying and singing hymns to God, and the prisoners were listening to them, and suddenly there was a great earthquake, so that the foundations of the prison were shaken. And immediately all the doors were opened, and everyone's bonds were unfastened. When the jailer woke and saw that the prison doors were open, he drew his sword and was about to kill himself, supposing that the prisoners had escaped. But Paul cried with a loud voice, "Do not harm yourself, for we are all here." And the jailer called for lights and rushed in, and trembling with fear he fell down before Paul and Silas. Then he brought them out and said, "Sirs, what must I do to be saved?" And they said, "Believe in the Lord Jesus, and you will be saved, you and your household." And they spoke the word of the Lord to him and to all who were in his house. And he took them the same hour of the night and washed their wounds; and he was baptized at once, he and all his family. Then he brought them up into his house and set food before them. And he rejoiced along with his entire household that he had believed in God.

Acts 16:25-34

Midnight. Chains. Bruised backs. A jail cell. And singing?

Paul and Silas were not giving a concert. They were offering worship in the dark. Their wounds still bled, and yet their mouths sang.

We do not always get to choose our circumstances. But we can choose our response.

Their praise pierced the silence, and God shook the prison. Not just the walls. The jailer's world, too. This hardened man, moments from taking his own life, finds hope in their song. And he asks, "What must I do to be saved?"

The answer is simple. "*Believe in the Lord Jesus.*" And that night, the jailer and his whole household found life.

What is stunning is that this church in Philippi, the one Paul later writes to about joy, was born in suffering, forged in praise, and founded on simple, saving faith.

When we sing in the dark, others hear. When we trust God in pain, people listen. And sometimes, it leads them straight to Jesus.

Father, when we are hurting, remind us that You are still good. Give us a song in the night. Use our faith to draw others to You.

We do not always get to choose our circumstances. But we can choose our response.

DAY 5
Godly Leverage

But when it was day, the magistrates sent the police, saying, "Let those men go." And the jailer reported these words to Paul, saying, "The magistrates have sent to let you go. Therefore come out now and go in peace." But Paul said to them, "They have beaten us publicly, uncondemned, men who are Roman citizens, and have thrown us into prison; and do they now throw us out secretly? No! Let them come themselves and take us out." The police reported these words to the magistrates, and they were afraid when they heard that they were Roman citizens. So they came and apologized to them. And they took them out and asked them to leave the city. So they went out of the prison and visited Lydia. And when they had seen the brothers, they encouraged them and departed.
Acts 16:35-40

The morning after the earthquake, the city officials try to smooth things over. Let them go quietly, they say. But Paul says, "No!"

He does not make a fuss to protect himself. He is thinking of someone else: the baby church in Philippi.

Paul was a Roman citizen, a privilege with real legal power. But instead of avoiding trouble, he used it to protect the vulnerable. His silence the night before glorified God, but his boldness now covers the church.

In his letter to the Philippians, Paul writes, "Live as citizens worthy of the gospel." Not Roman citizens, but Heavenly ones. He modeled it, choosing courage, wisdom, and protection for others over comfort for himself.

You and I may not live in first-century Philippi, but we have influence, rights, and voices. The question is: Will we use them for our own benefit or for the sake of others?

Citizenship is not just where we live; it is how we live. Let us leverage what we have been given to bless others.

Jesus, thank You for giving us a place in Your kingdom. Give us the courage to speak the truth and the wisdom to know when to act. Help us use every privilege or opportunity to protect, bless, and build up others in Your name. Let us live boldly, humbly, and wisely as citizens of heaven today.

Citizenship is not just where we live; it is how we live.

DAY 6
Work in Progress

And I am sure of this, that he who began a good work in you will bring it to completion at the day of Jesus Christ.
Philippians 1:6

What makes a letter timeless? It is not just the words on the page but the heart behind them. Paul's letter to the Philippians is more than ancient correspondence; it is a lifeline of encouragement from a man in chains to a church in a pagan, Roman outpost. And it still speaks.

Paul did not write from a beach house or retreat center. He wrote from prison, chained to a guard. Yet this letter pulses with joy. Paul is deeply thankful for this church: people like Lydia, the jailer, and others who came to Christ through hardship and miracles. And in his thankfulness, he reminds them: God is not done with you yet.

Have you ever wondered if your growth in Christ is stuck? Or felt like you have messed up one too many times? Hear Paul's promise clearly: God finishes what He starts. The same God who met us in our brokenness will grow us in grace. We do not have to manufacture fruit. God is the gardener.

As we open Philippians together, let this be our foundation: We are a work in progress, not a DIY project. God Himself is committed to our spiritual maturity. And His timeline? It is long, but perfect. Imagine the final reveal.

Lord, thank You for never giving up on us. Grow us in ways we cannot see. Remind us that You are always at work, even when we feel stuck. We trust You to finish what You started.

God finishes what He starts. The same God who met us in our brokenness will grow us in grace.

DAY 7
Amplifying the Gospel

I want you to know, brothers, that what has happened to me has really served to advance the gospel, so that it has become known throughout the whole imperial guard and to all the rest that my imprisonment is for Christ.
Philippians 1:12-13

It is easy to think that God can only use us when life is going well. But Paul flips that idea upside down. He's locked up, yet he writes about progress. How? For Paul, the gospel was never on pause; it just took on a different platform.

Paul's prison did not hinder the gospel; it amplified it. His guards heard about Jesus, and his fellow believers gained courage. The very thing that seemed to stop the mission became the stage for God's message.

Think about your "chains," that hard thing, that closed door, that struggle you did not choose. Could it be that God is using it to speak through you?

The world watches how we handle suffering. If we still trust God when things fall apart, our lives become testimonies. Like Paul, we begin to see purpose in pain, not because pain is good, but because God is.

Jesus, use the hard things in our lives for Your glory. Help us not to waste our challenges, difficulties, and suffering. Let us trust You with every chain and see Your hand in every circumstance.

DAY 8
Christian Compass

Have this mind among yourselves, which is yours in Christ Jesus, who, though he was in the form of God, did not count equality with God a thing to be grasped, but emptied himself, by taking the form of a servant, being born in the likeness of men. And being found in human form, he humbled himself by becoming obedient to the point of death, even death on a cross.
Philippians 2:5–8

If there is a heartbeat to Philippians, this is it. These verses are a poem, a hymn, and a theology class in just a few lines. They tell the story of Jesus, from glory to the grave. But more than that, they show us the shape of Christian life: one of downward humility before rising to glory.

In a culture that says "look out for yourself," Paul invites us to look at Christ. Jesus did not cling to His rights. He did not demand comfort. He came down. And the way up, in God's kingdom, is always through humble service and love.

Humility is not weakness. It is strength under control. It is choosing to serve when we demand authority. It is choosing to love when we could walk away. It is looking more like Jesus, little by little.

Let the cross be our compass as we begin this journey through Philippians. Let His humility shape how we lead, love, and live.

Lord Jesus, teach us to walk the downward path of humility. Help us to empty ourselves, not of value, but of pride. Let our lives echo Your love in the way we treat others today.

DAY 9
Life Redefined

But whatever gain I had, I counted as loss for the sake of Christ. Indeed, I count everything as loss because of the surpassing worth of knowing Christ Jesus my Lord. For his sake I have suffered the loss of all things and count them as rubbish, in order that I may gain Christ
Philippians 3:7–8

We live in a world obsessed with résumés, social status, and success stories. But Paul throws his spiritual résumé in the trash. Why? Because, compared to knowing Jesus, even the best of our achievements are just garbage.

Paul had pedigree, passion, and prestige. But when he met Christ, everything changed. Knowing Jesus was not just better; it redefined everything.

We can almost hear him saying: "All the trophies on my shelf? They don't hold a candle to the treasure I've found in Christ."

What do we count as gain? Is it grades, approval, popularity, or comfort? Paul challenges us to place all of it at the feet of Jesus, not because those things are evil, but because Jesus is infinitely better.

Following Jesus is not about giving up happiness; it is about finding real joy. It starts when we stop trying to prove ourselves and trust the One who already loves us.

Jesus, we confess that we often chase things that cannot satisfy. Help us to see You as our greatest treasure. Teach us to let go of what we do not need, so that we can hold onto You with both hands.

Knowing Jesus redefines everything.

DAY 10
In the Presence of Christ

Rejoice in the Lord always; again I will say, rejoice.
Philippians 4:4

Joy. It is not just a mood. It is not a reaction to an easy day or a full bank account. It is not a personality trait reserved for the naturally optimistic. According to the Apostle Paul, joy is a command. Not just once, but twice in one sentence. *"Rejoice in the Lord always; again I will say, rejoice."*

Rejoicing in the Lord is not wishful thinking. It is not naive or disconnected from reality. Paul wrote these words while chained to a Roman guard, imprisoned for preaching the gospel of Jesus Christ. His future is uncertain, his freedom is gone, and his critics are emboldened, yet he writes a letter brimming with joy. How?

Paul's joy was not tethered to circumstance. It was rooted in Christ. The Book of Philippians is not a shallow pep talk. It is a field manual for unshakable joy. It is a letter that teaches us how to think, live, serve, suffer, and walk with Christ in a way that transforms even our hardest seasons into opportunities for deep gladness in God. It is about finding joy when life makes no sense, because our Savior never changes.

Over the coming weeks, we will walk through this letter verse by verse. We will listen as Paul encourages his beloved church in Philippi. We will explore how gratitude, unity, humility, perseverance, and perspective are all integral to the joy-filled life God has designed for us. But before we dive in, we need to plant our flag in this truth:

Joy is found "*in the Lord*," not in the absence of problems but in the presence of Christ.

So, as we begin this study, ask: Where have I been looking for joy? Has it been in control, comfort, success, or others' approval? What if joy is not a destination to reach, but a person to know?

Lord, help me anchor my joy in You. Through Paul's letter, teach me how to rejoice always, not because life is easy, but because You are near, faithful, and enough. Let Your joy be my strength today and every day.

> *Joy is found "in the Lord," not in the absence of problems but in the presence of Christ.*

DAY 11
The Peace of God

Do not be anxious about anything, but in everything by prayer and supplication with thanksgiving let your requests be made known to God. And the peace of God, which surpasses all understanding, will guard your hearts and your minds in Christ Jesus.
Philippians 4:6–7

If you have ever struggled with anxiety, you are in good company. Paul wrote this from a jail cell, uncertain if he would live or die, and yet he tells us not to be anxious. Not because anxiety is sinful, but because we are not stuck with it.

His remedy is not complicated. It is not ten steps. It is one: *Pray.* And not just desperate, 2 a.m. prayers (though those are welcome). He says, *"Bring everything to God—with thanksgiving."*

Thanksgiving shifts the focus from what is wrong to who is in control. Prayer does not fix circumstances; it changes us. The peace of God does not always change our situation, but it *guards our hearts* right in the middle of it.

It is peace that does not make sense, quiet confidence when the world is loud, a holy calm when everything around us says panic. That is what Jesus offers.

So today, breathe. Pray. And let His peace hold you steady.

Father, we bring You every anxious thought. Remind us of who You are: strong, faithful, kind. We choose gratitude. We trust Your peace to guard our hearts and minds in Christ Jesus.

DAY 12
Reshaping Our Perspective

Grace to you and peace from God our
Father and the Lord Jesus Christ.
Philippians 1:2

The Book of Philippians begins like a warm letter from a friend. Paul, an apostle, church planter, and prisoner, writes from a Roman jail cell to a group of people he dearly loves: the believers in Philippi. Paul's letter is not a sterile theological treatise. It is a heartfelt message from a pastor to his people.

Before we dig into the verses, we need to understand the story behind the letter. Philippi was a Roman colony in Macedonia, a proud outpost of Roman culture. It was not a place steeped in Jewish tradition, but Paul was called there in a vision (**Acts 16**). There was no synagogue when he arrived; instead, he found a group of women praying by the river. From that quiet beginning came a remarkable church: Lydia, the first convert; a jailer and his family, saved after an earthquake; and others who formed a church full of Paul's most faithful and generous ministry partners.

Years later, Paul is in prison awaiting trial, uncertain of his future, and yet, instead of asking for help or comfort, he writes to encourage them. The theme? Joy in Christ. Again and again, Paul urges the Philippians to rejoice, stand firm, and live worthy of the gospel. Why? Because he knows that joy is not based on how things are going around us, but on who is alive within us.

Over the next few months, we will walk through this letter slowly, a few verses at a time. We will see how Paul's love for Christ and His church reshapes his view of suffering, relationships, success, and purpose.

So, take a deep breath. Open your heart. Let this be your journey, too.

Father, thank You for the story behind this letter. The initial meeting occurred by a river, in a prison, and through hardship. As we walk through Philippians, help us see what You want to teach us about joy, endurance, and the beauty of belonging to Christ.

Joy is not based on how things are going around us, but on who is alive within us.

DAY 13
Impressive Resume

Paul and Timothy, servants of Christ Jesus,

To all the saints in Christ Jesus who are at Philippi, with the overseers and deacons: Grace to you and peace from God our Father and the Lord Jesus Christ.
Philippians 1:1–2

When Paul opens his letter to the Philippians, he does not lead with his impressive résumé. No apostolic credentials. No spiritual superiority. Just this: *"Paul and Timothy, servants of Christ Jesus."*

That word *servants* is the Greek word *doulos,* literally *"slaves."* Not a flattering term. Not something any of us would list on our LinkedIn profiles. But for Paul, it was the most honored title he could claim: belonging to Jesus, bound to His will, joyfully surrendered to His service.

We live in a world that applauds fame and follows "influencers." People introduce themselves by what they do or what they have achieved. Paul, however, introduces himself by whose he is. That changes everything.

He is writing to *"all the saints in Christ Jesus,"* not just the pastors or the spiritually elite, but the whole church. From overseers to ordinary folks, from the pulpit to the pew, they all share the same identity: in Christ. In Christ is the great equalizer. If we are in Christ, we are saints, not because of our performance, but because of His grace.

How do we see ourselves? Is our worth tied to our job title, GPA, social status, or is it anchored in Christ? Have we embraced not only His forgiveness but also His call to follow, serve, and lay down our rights for the Gospel?

We do not have to strive for greatness in the world's eyes. We are already called, already chosen, already cherished. Like Paul, each of us is invited into a life of significance, not through the spotlight, but through servanthood.

Lord Jesus, teach us what it means to be Your servant. Quiet our craving for applause, and settle our hearts in the peace that comes from being Yours. May we serve today not out of duty, but out of delight. Let our lives echo Paul's: joyful, humble, surrendered.

If we are in Christ, we are saints, not because of our performance, but because of His grace.

DAY 14
Full-On Partnership

I thank my God in all my remembrance of you,
always in every prayer of mine for you all making
my prayer with joy, because of your partnership
in the gospel from the first day until now.
Philippians 1:3–5

Picture Paul in a dark Roman prison: chained, cold, and isolated. He is not complaining; he is not wallowing in self-pity. He is thanking God. With every memory of the Philippians, joy wells up in his heart. His prayers, even in confinement, are marked not by grief but by gratitude.

Why? *Because of their partnership in the gospel.*

Paul and the Church in Philippi had a shoulder-to-shoulder, heart-to-heart camaraderie in Christ. These believers were not casual fans of Paul's ministry. They were full-on partners. They gave, prayed, sent encouragement, and lived out the gospel in their city. Their bond with Paul was not based on geography. Their intimacy was built on shared purpose.

We often reduce fellowship to small talk over coffee or sitting in adjacent pews. But Paul paints a richer picture: fellowship as *mission-driven unity*. True Christian community is forged in the fires of shared calling. Deep relationships form when we roll up our sleeves, carry each other's burdens, and live for something greater than ourselves.

There is joy in that kind of togetherness. A joy that does not depend on circumstances. Joy that flows from knowing we are part of God's eternal work. Joy that reminds us we are not in it alone.

Are we spectators or partners in the gospel? Do our prayers include gratitude for the people God has placed beside us in ministry? Who are we laboring with for the sake of the Kingdom?

Father, thank You for the gift of gospel partnership. Thank You for the people who encourage us, challenge us, and walk with us in Your mission. Help us not to be content on the sidelines but to step into the work You have prepared for us. Let our lives be marked by joyful service and deep connection with Your people.

*True Christian community is forged
in the fires of shared calling.*

DAY 15
Not a DIY Project

And I am sure of this, that he who began a good work in you will bring it to completion at the day of Jesus Christ.
Philippians 1:6

Some mornings, we wake up wondering if we are making any progress at all. We still lose our temper, battle the same doubts, and feel like the person we were hoping to leave behind. In those moments, it is easy to believe the lie that nothing is happening and that God is finished with us.

But Paul states with a bold, Spirit-filled assurance: "*I am sure of this.*" Not wishful thinking. Not a vague hope. But a rock-solid certainty. "*He who began a good work in you.*" The God who saved us by grace, who loved us before we ever loved Him. "*Will bring it to completion.*"

> *Every stumble is not a sign of failure but a step in the process.*

The "*good work*" is not about us finally getting our act together. It is about God doing what only He can do: transforming our hearts, renewing our minds, and shaping us to look more like Jesus. Every stumble is not a sign of failure but a step in the process. The process is not in our hands. It is in His.

Embracing the truth that "*God finishes what He starts*" is both freeing and humbling. We are not the contractor. We are the construction site. Our job is not to finish the task but to yield to the One who can. Our stories are not over. We are not stuck. We are becoming.

We must remember that we are all works in progress. God is not finished. He is chiseling, shaping, and writing a story that ends in glory. From the moment of salvation, God has been shaping us. Every act of love, every step of faith, every struggle is utilized in His design.

Father, thank You for being faithful in finishing what You start. On the days we feel discouraged, remind us that You are still working. Help us trust the process, even when we do not see progress. Shape us into the people You have called us to be. Please give us the grace to wait while You build.

> *Our job is not to finish the task but to yield to the One who can.*

DAY 16
Partakers of Grace

It is right for me to feel this way about you all, because I hold you in my heart, for you are all partakers with me of grace, both in my imprisonment and in the defense and confirmation of the gospel. For God is my witness, how I yearn for you all with the affection of Christ Jesus.
Philippians 1:7–8

A powerful bond forms when people go through difficult experiences together. Soldiers in battle, parents in crisis, believers in trials, and teammates. They come out not just older or wiser, but closer to one another. That is the kind of love Paul is describing here.

Paul is not being polite or sentimental when he says, *"I hold you in my heart."* Why? These people did not run when things got hard. They stood beside him, not just in the sweet moments of shared victories, but in his suffering, his imprisonment, and the gritty work of defending the gospel. They were *partakers of grace,* not just recipients of it, but *sharers* in it.

Grace is the foundation of gospel friendship.

Grace is the foundation of gospel friendship. When we realize we are all broken people rescued by the same Savior, competition fades, and compassion rises. Suddenly, we do not have to prove ourselves. We just need to walk together, imperfect but covered.

Paul says he *yearns* for them with the affection of Christ Jesus. That is a divine, Spirit-filled love: selfless, sacrificial, and deeply personal. It is the kind of love Jesus has for us and wants to pour *through* us into the lives of others.

> *The affection of Christ is a divine, selfless, sacrificial, and deeply personal Spirit-filled love.*

Who are the grace partners in our lives? Who has walked with us in faith, in failure, in freedom? And who might need us to walk beside them now?

Jesus, thank You for the people who have stood with us in grace, the people who walked with us through joy and sorrow, victories and valleys. Help us love as You do, not just when it is easy, but when it is hard. Fill our hearts with genuine affection for those You have placed in our lives, and make us grace-givers, today and always.

DAY 17
Discerning Love

And it is my prayer that your love may abound more
and more, with knowledge and all discernment.
Philippians 1:9

Love is not a static feeling; it is something that grows. Paul's prayer for the Philippians is not that they would love *more*, but that they would love *better*.

We often think of love as an emotion: warm, fuzzy, compassionate. And love certainly includes kindness and tenderness. But biblical love is not blind affection. It is wise, rooted in truth, guided by God's Word, and anchored in Christ.

Paul prays for *abounding* love. A love that overflows, keeps growing, and never plateaus. However, it is a specific kind of love: love informed by *knowledge* and *discernment*. Why? Because not everything that appears to be love is genuinely beneficial. Sometimes, what feels kind can enable harm. Sometimes, what feels tough is the healing process.

> *Abounding love is informed by*
> *knowledge and discernment.*

Love without wisdom can lose its way. It might excuse sin in the name of acceptance or shy away from hard conversations in the name of peace. But love that is shaped by truth is strong enough to confront, tender enough to restore, and wise enough to know the difference.

God does not want our love to be shallow or aimless. He wants it to be patient, thoughtful, and active. For our love to abound, we must know His Word, listen to His Spirit, and be caring enough to ask, "*What is truly best for this person?*"

How is our love growing? Is it just emotional, or is it anchored in truth? Are we asking God for discernment as we love those around us?

Lord, we want to love wisely. Grow our love until it overflows with discernment and truth. Help us love like Jesus: with grace that heals and truth that sets free. Teach us when to speak, when to listen, when to act, and when to wait. Fill our hearts with wisdom-rooted love.

Love that is shaped by truth is strong enough to confront, tender enough to restore, and wise enough to know the difference.

DAY 18
Prepared for the Day

So that you may approve what is excellent, and
so be pure and blameless for the day of Christ,
Philippians 1:10

The more our love matures, the more our decisions mature as well. Approving what is excellent means choosing God's best, not just avoiding what is wrong. It is the difference between good and great, between permissible and purposeful.

Paul is praying for *love* to sharpen our *judgment*, so that our lives reflect what truly matters. It is the difference between choosing the urgent and choosing the eternal.

When our heart grows in love for Christ, our vision changes. We begin to see with spiritual clarity, like wiping fog off a mirror. Priorities shift. It is seeing life from God's perspective and choosing His best, even when it is costly.

The goal? A life that is *pure* (untainted by selfish motives) and *blameless* (a life that will not cause others to stumble).

Father, we want to live lives that reflect what matters most. Grow our love for You so that our decisions follow. Help us choose what is best, not what is easiest. Shape our hearts to pursue what is excellent, so we may be pure and blameless when we stand before You.

DAY 19
Healthy Fruit

*Filled with the fruit of righteousness
that comes through Jesus Christ...*
Philippians 1:11a

Ever try to force fruit out of a tree? It does not work. Fruit is the natural result of a healthy tree. In the same way, righteousness is not manufactured; it is grown through a life rooted in Christ.

Paul says the fruit of righteousness comes through Jesus. It is not about doing more and trying harder. It is about staying close to Jesus and letting Him shape our lives from the inside out.

Trying to live the Christian life apart from Christ is like tying oranges to a fence and calling it a grove. It may look good for a moment, but it does not last. Real fruit comes from abiding.

So, how do we stay rooted in Christ? Through His Word, where He speaks. Through prayer, where we commune with Him. Through His people, where we grow in grace and accountability. The more connected we are, the more fruit appears; often quietly, gradually, but unmistakably.

And this fruit? It is not for show, it is for sharing. Love, joy, peace, patience, kindness....**(Galatians 5:22-23)** All are meant to nourish the lives around us.

Jesus, help us stay rooted in You. We do not want to live lives of performance. We want lives that overflow. Grow in us the fruit of righteousness. Let love and goodness flow from our lives, not because we strive, but because we remain in You.

But the fruit of the Spirit is love, joy, peace, patience, kindness, goodness, faithfulness, gentleness, self-control; against such things there is no law.
Galatians 5:22-23

DAY 20
A Window for Praise

Filled with the fruit of righteousness that comes through
Jesus Christ, to the glory and praise of God.
Philippians 1:11

Why does love that grows, discernment that sharpens, and righteousness that bears fruit matter? Because it brings glory and praise not to us, but to God.

Paul does not just tack this phrase on like a signature. It is the reason for everything he prayed: that God would be glorified through our lives.

Imagine our everyday decisions, our unseen faithfulness, our quiet acts of love becoming a living doxology. A song of praise that rises from our lives to the throne of heaven.

We were not created to build personal platforms or chase applause. We were made to reflect the brilliance of our Creator. When our lives radiate grace, when our choices reflect wisdom, and when our character bears the mark of Jesus, our lives become a window for others to see how good God is.

We were not made just to survive; we were made to glorify. Whether we are parenting, teaching, suffering, forgiving, or leading, remember it is all worship.

God, we want our lives to be a shining light that draws others to You. Use our words, our work, our love, and even our struggles to bring You praise. May the story of our lives make Your name famous.

DAY 21
A Setup for Something More

I want you to know, brothers, that what has happened to me has really served to advance the gospel, so that it has become known throughout the whole imperial guard and to all the rest that my imprisonment is for Christ. And most of the brothers, having become confident in the Lord by my imprisonment, are much more bold to speak the word without fear.
Philippians 1:12-14

Paul's prison cell did not appear to be a sign of progress. Chains clanked where pulpit words once rang out. But he was not discouraged. Why? Because Paul had learned a secret that changes everything: when Christ is preached, even suffering becomes a victory.

The gospel was not chained because Paul was. Soldiers in Caesar's elite guard were hearing the message of Jesus firsthand. Paul's courage emboldened timid and unsure fellow believers. What looked like a setback was a setup for gospel advance.

> *What looked like a setback was a setup for gospel advance.*

What if we viewed our setbacks in the same way? That frustrating job? The painful diagnosis? The relationship struggle? Paul teaches us to look for the gospel's advance in the middle of challenges. God is not wasting your suffering. He is using it.

Joy is not found in a pain-free life. Joy is found when our pain has a purpose. Paul's purpose was clear: whether free or imprisoned, his life was to make Christ known. The result? Even his chains sang praise.

God is not wasting your suffering. He is using it.

Today, ask: What if this pain is part of God's plan to spread His hope? Someone is watching how we respond and gaining courage because of it?

Lord, use our trials to glorify You. Help us see that even in confinement, You are advancing the good news. May our suffering, struggles, and situations serve as a testimony that strengthens others.

DAY 22
The Progress of the Gospel

Some indeed preach Christ from envy and rivalry, but others from good will. The latter do it out of love, knowing that I am put here for the defense of the gospel. The former proclaim Christ out of selfish ambition, not sincerely but thinking to afflict me in my imprisonment. What then? Only that in every way, whether in pretense or in truth, Christ is proclaimed, and in that I rejoice. Yes, and I will rejoice.
Philippians 1:15-18

Paul's honesty is refreshing. He admits some people are preaching Christ with impure motives, such as envy, rivalry, maybe even hoping to rub salt in his wounds while he is in prison. But Paul does not take the bait. He says, *"Christ is proclaimed, and in that I rejoice."*

That is a rare kind of freedom. Most of us are deeply affected by other people's intentions. We want to be recognized for what we do, appreciated for how we lead, and defended when others try to undercut us. But Paul was driven by something more important: the progress of the gospel, not the politics of people.

He could rejoice not because people were kind or fair, but because Jesus was being proclaimed. The message mattered more than the messengers. How liberating would it be to care less about what people say about us, and more about what they say about Jesus?

Yes, impure motives hurt. Paul did not deny that. But he lifted his eyes above the drama to something eternal: God is still using it. And that was reason enough to rejoice.

Father, help us rise above petty comparisons and selfish ambition. Teach us to find joy in the simple truth that Christ is being made known, even when others seek their own gain. Make Your glory our goal.

DAY 23
Not Solutions, Faith

For I know that through your prayers and the help of the Spirit of Jesus Christ this will turn out for my deliverance, as it is my eager expectation and hope that I will not be at all ashamed, but that with full courage now as always Christ will be honored in my body, whether by life or by death.
Philippians 1:19-20

Prison was not the end of Paul's story. It was a page in God's bigger book. And Paul had a confident expectation: this suffering would lead to his deliverance. Not necessarily a release from jail, but a refining of faith.

Paul was not hoping in Rome. He was hoping in Christ. He knew the Spirit of Jesus would not abandon him. And he knew the prayers of the church were powerful. Together, those two forces of prayer and the Spirit sustained him in the waiting.

We have all experienced difficult situations, unsure of the outcome, and uncertain about what the process entailed. Paul gives us a model for those moments. He does not demand answers. He asks for the faith not to be put to shame. Whether he lived or died, he wanted Christ to be honored.

That is a different kind of deliverance. It is not an escape. It is endurance. It is not avoiding the fire. It is being refined by it.

When God's people pray and the Spirit strengthens them, even prison becomes a place of peace. What if we stopped asking for the trial to end and started asking for Christ to be honored through it?

Jesus, thank You for hearing us in the waiting. Help us not to waste the trial, but to grow through it. We trust that You will be glorified in us, whether by life or by death.

DAY 24
Joy Flows from Surrender

For to me to live is Christ, and to die is gain.
Philippians 1:21

With these words, Paul offers a reorientation of how to view life and death. To Paul, both were opportunities. Life meant fruitful labor for Christ. Death meant being with Christ. Either way, Christ was the prize.

That kind of surrender does not come naturally. Most of us grip tightly to our plans, our comfort, our goals. We worry. We strategize. We try to hold it all together. But Paul had already let go. His life was not his own. His life belonged entirely to Jesus. And when we live like that, we are no longer afraid. We are not reckless, but we are free. Free from fear. Free from needing control. Free to truly live.

Paul was not giving up on life. He was not despondent or weary. He understood what mattered most. Eternity was not a distant idea; it was the finish line, the fulfillment. Until then, he was dedicated to the mission of helping others grow in their faith and joy. That is the heart of gospel living.

Joy takes root, not in getting what we want, but in giving ourselves away. The secret of the Christian life is believing joy flows from surrender and submission. When we embrace this truth, we stop asking, "What's best for me?" and begin asking, "What will bring the most glory to Jesus?"

Lord, help us live today with eternity in view. Let our time on earth bring joy to others and honor to You. Whether in life or death, may Christ be magnified in us.

DAY 25
Investing for Eternity

If I am to live in the flesh, that means fruitful labor for me. Yet which I shall choose I cannot tell. I am hard pressed between the two. My desire is to depart and be with Christ, for that is far better. But to remain in the flesh is more necessary on your account. Convinced of this, I know that I will remain and continue with you all, for your progress and joy in the faith, so that in me you may have ample cause to glory in Christ Jesus, because of my coming to you again.
Philippians 1:22-26

Paul was caught between two holy desires: to be with Christ or to continue serving His people. One sounded like heaven, while the other required sacrifice. But Paul chose the more challenging path because of his love for people.

Paul believed that his staying and continuing his ministry was not about self-preservation, but about the progress of others. He did not say, "*I guess I'll hang on for a bit longer.*" He said, "*I will remain for your joy.*"

The heart of Christ living in Paul is the love that chooses service over comfort, mission over escape, investment over isolation. It is the kind of love that says, "*As long as I'm breathing, I'm here to build you up.*"

What would it look like if we lived that way? If we saw each day not as something to survive, but as a God-given opportunity to strengthen someone else's faith? Our presence, our faith, our example, our words might be the very thing God uses to help someone else move forward.

Paul's great joy was not just in being with Christ, but in helping others grow into Him. So, if we are still here, there is still a purpose. Someone needs our faithfulness. Someone needs encouragement. Someone needs an example of what it means to walk with Jesus through both difficult and good times, with a heart full of joy. Let that be our reason for staying.

> *The heart of Christ living in us is the love that chooses service over comfort, mission over escape, investment over isolation.*

Father, thank You for the days You've given us. Help us use each one to strengthen someone else's faith. Give us eyes to see who needs hope today and a heart ready to serve them for Your glory.

DAY 26
One Thing

Only let your manner of life be worthy of the gospel of Christ, so that whether I come and see you or am absent, I may hear of you that you are standing firm in one spirit, with one mind striving side by side for the faith of the gospel
Philippians 1:27

Paul boils it down to one big thing, just one. Live life in a way that reflects the worth of the gospel. Do not just talk about it. Do not simply agree with it. Live it. This is a call to citizenship. Paul is using language that Roman Philippians would understand: behave like a citizen who honors the name you carry. For us, that name is Christ.

Living "*worthy*" does not mean earning God's love or proving our worthiness. We could never do that. The gospel is grace through and through. But once we have received it, our lives should echo its beauty. Our words, our work, our reactions, and our relationships should all speak of the value of the One who saved us.

> Our words, our work, our reactions, and our relationships should all speak of the value of the One who saved us.

It is easy to reduce Christianity to Sunday services and private beliefs. However, Paul pushes deeper. If we believe the gospel is of infinite value, then our lives should reflect that value daily. When we forgive instead of retaliating, serve instead of demanding, and hope instead of despairing, we show what Christ is worth to us.

> *If we believe the gospel is of infinite value, then our lives should reflect that value daily.*

This verse invites us to inspect our lives. Are we showing that Jesus is worthy? Are we living like citizens of heaven, loyal to His kingdom and its values? Or are we blending in with the crowd?

The gospel changes not just what we believe, but how we behave. Paul says, *"Let your whole life match the message of Christ."*

Father, help us live today in a way that shows how much You are worth. Let our words and actions reflect the beauty of the gospel. Make our lives a living testimony of grace, truth, and love.

DAY 27
Steadfast Unity

Only let your manner of life be worthy of the gospel of Christ, so that whether I come and see you or am absent, I may hear of you that you are standing firm in one spirit, with one mind striving side by side for the faith of the gospel
Philippians 1:27

Paul paints a picture of a unified body standing strong together. Imagine soldiers locked arm in arm, holding the line against an advancing army. That is the church when it lives worthy of the gospel.

Our culture values independence, but the gospel calls us to interdependence. Paul does not say *"stand firm on your own."* He says, *"side by side."* You and I are not meant to walk this road alone.

> *Unity does not mean sameness;*
> *it means shared purpose.*

Sadly, too many Christians go it alone or worse, fight each other instead of the real enemy. Division kills momentum. When we compete instead of cooperating, the mission suffers. But when we strive together with one mind, one goal, and one heart, we reflect the unity of Christ.

What makes steadfast unity possible? A shared focus: the gospel. We rally around Christ, not our preferences. Our common mission is to make Him known, not make ourselves comfortable.

Paul challenges us to get our eyes off ourselves and onto the mission. Are we walking in step with other believers? Are we helping others stand firm? Or have we been more focused on what we are not getting?

Our common mission is to make Him known, not make ourselves comfortable.

Unity does not mean sameness; it means shared purpose. And it is one of the clearest signs that the gospel is real in our lives.

Lord, bind us together with our brothers and sisters in Christ. Help us stand firm, not in pride or independence, but in love and unity. Let us strive side by side for the gospel, encouraging one another, building up, and advancing Your kingdom together.

DAY 28
Granted to Suffer

And not frightened in anything by your opponents. This is a clear sign to them of their destruction, but of your salvation, and that from God. For it has been granted to you that for the sake of Christ you should not only believe in him but also suffer for his sake, engaged in the same conflict that you saw I had and now hear that I still have.
Philippians 1:28-30

It almost sounds like a mistake: *granted* to suffer? Paul says that suffering for Christ is not a punishment, but a privilege. God has given it, not as a curse, but as a gift.

Believing that the Lord grants suffering cuts against our instincts. Most of us work hard to avoid pain. But Paul sees suffering as something sacred. It is proof that we belong to Jesus. It is a sign, not of God's neglect, but of His nearness.

When we suffer for our faith, whether through rejection, ridicule, or loss, we are following in the footsteps of Jesus. We are living a life worthy of the gospel. The Lord does not waste the pain and trials; He transforms the suffering into an act of worship.

Suffering tests what we treasure.

Suffering tests what we treasure. Do we love comfort more than Christ? Do we value ease more than eternal reward? Paul reminds us that just as Christ suffered for us, we now get to suffer for Him, and in doing so, declare His supreme worth.

We often think faith is about what we get. Paul says it is about what we give, even if that means pain. But here is the promise: our suffering is never alone, never wasted, and never forgotten. It is a clear sign of our salvation and His kingdom.

Jesus, thank You for the gift of suffering, not because it is easy, but because it brings us closer to You. Help us endure with joy, knowing that we are sharing in Your mission and showing Your worth to the world.

Suffering for Christ is a sacred act in which we declare His supreme worth.

DAY 29
Encourage Others

So if there is any encouragement in Christ, any comfort from love, any participation in the Spirit, any affection and sympathy, complete my joy by being of the same mind, having the same love, being in full accord and of one mind.
Philippians 2:1–2

Paul's words are a gentle nudge: "If Christ has meant anything to you, then let it show in your unity." His logic is simple. Has Jesus encouraged you? Then encourage others. Have you tasted God's comfort? Then offer comfort. Have you been drawn into the fellowship of the Spirit? Then preserve that fellowship with others.

Paul is pointing to the unity of a shared mindset rooted in gospel love. "Be of the same mind," he says. Having the same mind is not about liking the same music or agreeing on every issue. It is about having a humble posture, demonstrating Christ-centered love, and pursuing Spirit-fueled goals together.

Unity is the fruit of hearts softened by grace. When we focus on Christ and not ourselves, when we remember what we have received, it changes how we treat each other, bringing joy to God and others.

Lord, thank You for the encouragement, love, and fellowship You have poured into our lives. Help us live in unity with others. Soften our hearts to be more like Yours. Empower us with your Spirit to demonstrate grace and affection.

DAY 30
If Any

So if there is any encouragement in Christ, any comfort from love, any participation in the Spirit, any affection and sympathy, complete my joy by being of the same mind, having the same love, being in full accord and of one mind.
Philippians 2:1–2

Even a little is enough.

If we have tasted even the tiniest sip of Christ's encouragement... If we have caught just a glimpse of comfort from His love...If we have shared even a moment in step with the Spirit... If we have felt the faintest flicker of His affection or sympathy, then we have enough to love others like Jesus.

Paul is not piling on pressure; he is stirring up perspective. He is not saying, "Do better!" He is asking, "Haven't you received something from God?" Of course, we have. Even on our worst days, His grace has not run dry. We may not feel strong, but we have more in us than we think, because He is in us.

> *Even on our worst days, His grace has not run dry.*

And that "*any*" is the fuel. Where has God met us recently with "*just enough*," and how might He use "*any*" to encourage someone else today?

God takes the small and multiplies it. A tiny mustard seed of faith moves mountains. A few loaves feed thousands. A flicker of encouragement, a whisper of love, a moment of fellowship. God can build a community out of that.

Paul says, "*Complete my joy.*" Pull together. Be one. Not through human effort, but through divine overflow. The same comfort we have received. Pass it on. The encouragement Christ gave us. Offer it freely. Let what God has given us bind us to the people around us.

> *A flicker of encouragement, a whisper of love, a moment of fellowship. God can build a community out of that.*

Lord, thank You that even the smallest touch of Your grace is more than enough. Remind us of how comforted, encouraged, and walked with us. Help us live out of that overflow, extending love, unity, and compassion to others.

DAY 31
Nothing

Do nothing from selfish ambition or conceit, but in humility count others more significant than yourselves.
Philippians 2:3

Selfish ambition is sneaky. It masks itself in confidence, but underneath it thrives on pushing ahead, climbing over others, and craving praise. Conceit *(empty glory)* chases applause and ends in pride. Paul calls it out with force: *"Nothing from selfish ambition!"* Not *"some things."* **"Nothing."**

Then comes the hard command: *"Count others more significant than yourselves."* It is not about whether they deserve it. It is a choice to esteem, to consider, to value. It is laying aside the spotlight and lifting others up.

Imagine how our homes, schools, workplaces, or churches would feel if everyone put others first. That kind of humility is not natural; it is a supernatural quality. And it begins in the heart.

Jesus did not seek applause. He sought obedience. That is our call too. A life of unity starts when we dethrone ourselves and enthrone Christ.

We must ask ourselves, *"How can I honor someone above myself?"* It might be letting someone else speak first, forgiving a minor offense, or serving without being noticed. When we humble ourselves, we walk in the footsteps of Jesus.

Jesus, You gave up glory to serve. Teach us to let go of selfish ambition. Help us to truly see others, value them, serve them, and count them more significant than ourselves.

DAY 32
Look

Let each of you look not only to his own interests,
but also to the interests of others.
Philippians 2:4

Paul says, "Look beyond yourself." The world says, "Look out for number one." Christ says, "Look out for others." This verse does not tell us to neglect ourselves; instead, it encourages us to open our eyes to others as well.

To "*look*" means intentional attention. It is an invitation to widen our vision. What if our homes, workplaces, and churches became places where people actively looked out for one another? This kind of "*look*" happens when a parent sees their child's silent struggle. The friend who asks the second question. The believer who gives, serves, and notices.

Imagine how freeing it would be if we knew someone else had our back, because we had theirs. What if we worked and worshipped in places where every person showed up asking, "How can I help?" That is a gospel-shaped community. A place where people lay down their self-focus to lift each other up. When we live this way, people see Jesus in us and experience the fragrant aroma of Christ.

Our world is hurting. People are weary. And sometimes, the most powerful ministry is simply seeing others and choosing to care for them.

Father, open our eyes to the needs around us. Help us lift our gaze from our own world and look for ways to serve, love, and encourage others today.

DAY 33
You Already Have It

Have this mind among yourselves,
which is yours in Christ Jesus
Philippians 2:5

Paul says, "Think like Jesus. Live like Jesus. Let His mindset become yours." This is not about mimicking Christ from a distance. It is about allowing His Spirit to shape how we perceive ourselves, others, and our place in the world.

Jesus' mindset was shaped by humility, service, and surrender. He did not cling to His rights. He gave them up. He did not demand honor. He embraced obscurity. He did not avoid suffering. He chose to accept human challenges out of love.

This mindset is "yours in Christ Jesus." We do not have to manufacture it. If we belong to Him, we have His Spirit, and His Spirit is forming His mind in us. His Spirit gives us a new way of thinking, a new lens through which we see ourselves and others. We do not have to fight for position or recognition when we know we are already seated with Christ.

When humility feels unnatural, remember that we already possess the mind of Christ. Now, live like it. The next time pride flares up or self-interest takes center stage, pause and pray, "Lord, give me Your mind. Shape my heart like Yours."

Jesus, we want to think like You, love like You, and live like You. Remind us that Your mindset is already ours through the Spirit. Make us more like You: humble, kind, and surrendered.

DAY 34
Letting Go in Order to Love More

Who (Jesus), though he was in the form of God, did not count equality with God a thing to be grasped, but emptied himself, by taking the form of a servant, being born in the likeness of men. And being found in human form, he humbled himself by becoming obedient to the point of death, even death on a cross.
Philippians 2:6–8

Jesus had every right to stay in heaven's glory. He was and is God. But He did not cling to His status. He let go, stepped down, and took on flesh. And not just any flesh, a servant's flesh. Then He went lower still, humbling Himself to die on a cross.

Why? For you. For me. For love.

The scandal and wonder of the gospel is that the highest became the lowest so the lowest could be lifted up. Paul says, Let Christ's life shape us. Let the story of Christ's humility break our pride. Let it soften our grip on our rights. Let it drive us to love more freely and serve with greater joy.

Because when we see how far He went for us, no act of obedience feels too small in return.

Jesus, thank You for humbling Yourself for us. Forgive us when we cling to pride. Teach us to walk in obedience, even when it costs us, because You are worth it.

DAY 35
Fully Empty

Who (Jesus), though he was in the form of God, did not count equality with God a thing to be grasped, but emptied himself, by taking the form of a servant, being born in the likeness of men. And being found in human form, he humbled himself by becoming obedient to the point of death, even death on a cross.
Philippians 2:6–8

These verses are sacred ground. Paul lifts the curtain on the humility of Christ. Jesus chose not to stay enthroned in heaven, surrounded by worship. But He gave up His rights; not His deity, but His privileges, and stepped into our world.

He "*emptied himself.*" Not by losing divinity, but by pouring out love. He chose servanthood over status. He willingly wrapped Himself in flesh and walked among the broken.

The heart of the gospel is that the King became a servant. God put on skin. He entered our mess to save us. He is our model. When we are tempted to cling to position, comfort, or recognition, Christ whispers, "*Follow me. Serve. Love.*"

Lord Jesus, You let go of everything for us. Help us let go of pride, selfishness, and the pursuit of status. Teach us the joy of serving. Let our lives reflect Your self-giving love.

DAY 36
Intentional Obedience

Who (Jesus), though he was in the form of God,
did not count equality with God a thing to be grasped,
but emptied himself, by taking the form of a servant,
being born in the likeness of men. And being found in
human form, he humbled himself by becoming obedient
to the point of death, even death on a cross.
Philippians 2:6-8

Jesus did not just visit Earth; He descended, not as a king in splendor but as a servant in humility. Paul's description of Christ should make us pause: the eternal Son of God, wrapped in human flesh, not to be admired but to be crucified.

Jesus did not hold onto His rights. He let go. He did not insist on comfort or safety. He endured pain. He did not grasp at honor. He embraced a criminal's death. Death on a cross, the most humiliating, shameful, torturous death of all.

Why would He do this?

Love.

Love that obeys the Father, even when it costs everything. Love that stoops; not because it is weak, but because it is strong enough to carry our sin.

Jesus chose to walk the hard road. He chose the cross. And He chose each one of us.

So the question echoes: Will we humble ourselves in return? Will we obey when it is costly, love when it is inconvenient, and serve when no one's watching?

Jesus chose to walk the hard road.
He chose the cross. And He chose each one of us.

Jesus, You gave up more than we can comprehend so we could be raised to life. Forgive us for clinging to our rights or our pride. Teach us to walk in Your footsteps. Walking with humility, obedience, and love. Help us to choose the cross-shaped path, trusting that resurrection always follows surrender.

DAY 37
Destination Fueled by Love

And being found in human form, he humbled himself by becoming obedient to the point of death, even death on a cross. Therefore God has highly exalted him and bestowed on him the name that is above every name, so that at the name of Jesus every knee should bow, in heaven and on earth and under the earth, and every tongue confess that Jesus Christ is Lord, to the glory of God the Father.
Philippians 2:8–11

Jesus did not stop at humility. He went to the cross. The King of glory obeyed even when it led to agony. He submitted to the grave. His death was not an accident. It was the destination of His love.

His humiliation became His exaltation. Because He lived in submission, God lifted Him high. The cross led to the crown. Sacrifice led to supreme honor. And now every knee will bow, and every tongue confess that Jesus Christ is Lord.

What does this mean for us? It means the way up is down. In God's kingdom, the humble are lifted. Those who serve will be honored. The road to greatness runs through sacrifice.

Do not chase applause. Do not cling to comfort. Follow the One who knelt to serve, died to save, and now reigns forever.

Jesus, You were obedient to the point of death, and now You are exalted above all. Help us follow Your example. Let our lives be shaped by Your cross and fueled by the hope of resurrection glory.

DAY 38
Humility Leads to Honor

Therefore, God has highly exalted him and bestowed on him the name that is above every name, so that at the name of Jesus every knee should bow, in heaven and on earth and under the earth, and every tongue confess that Jesus Christ is Lord, to the glory of God the Father.
Philippians 2:9-11

Because He emptied Himself and fully obeyed the Father, God exalted Him above all, giving Him the highest name, the highest honor, the highest praise.

One day, every knee will bow. Every voice will acknowledge His greatness. But do not wait until then. Start now. Let your life declare: Jesus is Lord.

When we follow His path of humility, God lifts us up as well, not for our glory, but for His. The way up is always down. Surrender leads to joy. Humility leads to honor.

So, live to lift up the name that is above every name. Bow your heart today and say, *"Jesus, You are Lord of all, including me."*

Father, we bow before You and exalt the name of Jesus. He is worthy. He is Lord. Help us live in surrender and awe, knowing that true greatness comes through humility.

DAY 39
Work it Out

Therefore, my beloved, as you have always obeyed, so now, not only as in my presence but much more in my absence, work out your own salvation with fear and trembling
Philippians 2:12

We are not instructed to earn our salvation; Paul is telling us to live it out. Like a seed that must grow into a tree, salvation begins in the heart but must bloom into action. We do not obey to get God's approval; we obey because we have it.

"Fear and trembling" does not mean terror; it means reverence. It is the awe of knowing God is at work in us. It is the humility of recognizing our weakness and the majesty of His power.

Paul's audience had obeyed in the past, but they needed to continue, whether Paul was present or not. Obedience is not a performance for others. It is a posture of the heart before God.

Keep walking. Keep growing. Keep working out what God has worked in. And do it with a heart that trembles with wonder.

Lord, help us to live out the salvation You have given us. Give us the courage to obey even when no one's watching. Let our lives reflect the awe and reverence we feel for You.

DAY 40
I Want to Want to

For it is God who works in you,
both to will and to work for his good pleasure.
Philippians 2:13

A life of obedience is not about our effort; it is about God's presence. The Lord not only gives us the ability to act, but He also provides the desire to obey. He changes our "*want to.*"

Jesus is personally invested in our growth. He is working in us, shaping our will, energizing our actions. Every step of faith is backed by infinite grace.

We are not running on willpower. We are running on resurrection power. When obedience is difficult and the "*want to*" no longer seems to be there, do not give up. Lean into grace. God is doing something beautiful in us, for His pleasure, and for our joy.

Father, thank You for working in us. When we are weak, You are strong. When we hesitate, You supply desire. Keep shaping our hearts and empowering our steps. We want to live for Your pleasure.

DAY 41
Fuel Endurance

Do all things without grumbling or disputing, that you may be blameless and innocent, children of God without blemish in the midst of a crooked and twisted generation, among whom you shine as lights in the world, holding fast to the word of life.
Philippians 2:14-16

Grumbling is a quiet rebellion. It whispers, "*God isn't doing enough.*" Disputing stirs division. And Paul says: eliminate both. Why? Because they dim our light.

The world is full of complaints. But joy is rare. Contentment is contagious. Gratitude stands out. When we choose joy over grumbling and unity over division, we become radiant, like stars against a dark sky.

How do we do it? We cling to the Word. "*Hold fast to the word of life,*" Paul says. Scripture steadies our hearts. It reminds us of God's goodness and fuels our endurance.

Our attitude is part of our witness. A thankful, faithful life is a glowing testimony in a broken world.

Lord, forgive us for the times we have grumbled instead of trusted. Help us to shine with joy, gratitude, and peace. Let Your Word anchor us so we can reflect Your light to those around us.

DAY 42
Shine

Do all things without grumbling or disputing, that you may be blameless and innocent, children of God without blemish in the midst of a crooked and twisted generation, among whom you shine as lights in the world, holding fast to the word of life.
Philippians 2:14-16

What makes us shine? It is not flashy words or perfect lives. It is the quiet, consistent glow of Christlike character. It is when we live without constant complaining, when we stop fighting over petty things, when we choose peace over pettiness, humility over harshness, obedience over convenience.

That is what Paul means when he says, "*Do all things without grumbling or disputing.*" Because when we do, we stand out. We become "blameless and innocent," not because we are flawless, but because we are different, set apart, reshaped by grace.

We do not have to shout to shine. We just have to hold fast to the Word of life. Keep showing up. Keep choosing kindness. Keep living like Jesus matters, because He does.

The world does not need more noise. It needs more light.

Consider those places where we are tempted to grumble or argue. How might choosing a different response help us shine more brightly for Christ?

Father, in a world that is dark and divided, help us to be different. Teach us to live without grumbling, to love without arguing, and to hold fast to Your Word. Make us shine for Your sake.

DAY 43
It Mattered

Do all things without grumbling or disputing, that you may be blameless and innocent, children of God without blemish in the midst of a crooked and twisted generation, among whom you shine as lights in the world, holding fast to the word of life, so that in the day of Christ I may be proud that I did not run in vain or labor in vain.
Philippians 2:14-16

Paul longed to know that his ministry bore fruit, not for personal glory, but because eternal things matter. He did not want to look back and see wasted effort. He wanted to stand before Christ with joy, knowing that the people he loved were walking in truth.

The heart of a spiritual parent is to see their children continue in what they have learned. Paul poured himself out so others could know Jesus more deeply. His hope? That their faithful lives would validate his sacrifice.

We can easily lose sight of the big picture. Every act of obedience, every moment we invest in others, every word of encouragement, it all counts. Eternity is watching. Keep going. Run the race in a way that brings joy to others. Our lives should be part of someone else's reward, and we must make sure theirs is part of ours.

Lord, we want to live lives that count. Help us invest in people in a way that lasts. Strengthen us to run faithfully and love deeply, so that none of it is in vain.

DAY 44
Poured Out

Even if I am to be poured out as a drink offering upon the sacrificial offering of your faith, I am glad and rejoice with you all. Likewise you also should be glad and rejoice with me.
Philippians 2:17-18

"Poured out" is not a casual phrase. It is the language of sacrifice. Of emptying oneself for the sake of others. It echoes the Old Testament imagery of a drink offering, a final, costly pour over the altar, an act of devotion.

Paul's message is not: "Feel sorry for me, I am suffering." He says, *"Even if my life is spent for your growth in Christ, I rejoice."* And then he adds, *"Likewise... you should rejoice too."*

Why? Because there is joy in living for something bigger than ourselves. Joy in pouring out our energy, our time, our comfort, and even our very lives for the sake of someone else's faith.

The world teaches us to protect, preserve, and pursue self-fulfillment. But the gospel invites us into a deeper kind of joy. A contagious joy that grows when we surrender our rights, serve others, and give ourselves away.

Perhaps *"pouring out"* today means parenting through exhaustion, mentoring someone younger in the faith, or serving in a way that no one sees. Do not underestimate the impact. God watches. And heaven rejoices.

Father, thank You for the example of Paul, who poured out his life for others. Teach us to serve with that same heart. Help us rejoice, even in the sacrifice, knowing You use it all for Your glory.

DAY 45
Glad to Give

Even if I am to be poured out as a drink offering upon the sacrificial offering of your faith, I am glad and rejoice with you all. Likewise you also should be glad and rejoice with me.
Philippians 2:17-18

The mental image of the wine pouring from the cup over a sacrifice proclaiming forgiveness and redemption was the final fragrant expression of worship in the temple. Paul illustrates his desire for Christ followers to understand the joy of being entirely spent serving others, so that they may experience grace and forgiveness, and grow in faith.

The heart of joyful sacrifice is not begrudging, not bitter, but glad to give. The world tells us to hold on, protect, and preserve. But Jesus calls us to pour out for His glory and others' good. True joy often comes not from gaining, but giving. Serving. Sacrificing.

Paul says, "*Likewise, you too.*" Live open-handed. Let your lives be an offering. And rejoice. He invites the Philippians to join him: "*You also should be glad and rejoice with me.*" When sacrifice is done in love, it is not loss; it is worship.

We rejoice because our lives and our actions are rooted in the greater story of God's redemptive work. When we offer ourselves to God as living sacrifices (**Romans 12:1**), our joy is anchored not in what we have or what we achieve, but in Christ who is at work through us.

Jesus, help us pour ourselves out for others, not with a sigh, but with a smile. Teach us to live generously and joyfully. Let our lives be poured out in love, just as Yours was for us.

DAY 46
Always Showing Up

I hope in the Lord Jesus to send Timothy to you soon, so that I too may be cheered by news of you. For I have no one like him, who will be genuinely concerned for your welfare. For they all seek their own interests, not those of Jesus Christ. But you know Timothy's proven worth, how as a son with a father he has served with me in the gospel. I hope therefore to send him just as soon as I see how it will go with me, and I trust in the Lord that shortly I myself will come also.
Philippians 2:19-24

Timothy was not flashy, famous, or forceful. But he was faithful. And that made all the difference.

Paul says, "*I have no one like him.*" What made Timothy stand out? He genuinely cared for people. He was not in it for himself. He was not climbing a ladder. He simply served with love, loyalty, and consistency.

That is what Paul calls "*proven worth.*" In a world that values image and instant results, God values faithfulness. People who show up, who care, and who put others first are those who stand out in God's depth chart.

We do not need to be famous to matter in the kingdom. We need to be faithful. Timothy's life reminds us: the greatest servants are often quietly doing the most eternal work.

Father, help us to be faithful like Timothy. Let us care deeply and serve humbly. We may never be well-known, but let us be well-used for Your glory.

DAY 47
Running After Christ

I hope in the Lord Jesus to send Timothy to you soon, so that I too may be cheered by news of you. For I have no one like him, who will be genuinely concerned for your welfare. For they all seek their own interests, not those of Jesus Christ. But you know Timothy's proven worth, how as a son with a father he has served with me in the gospel. I hope, therefore, to send him as soon as I see how it will go with me, and I trust in the Lord that shortly I myself will come also.
Philippians 2:19-24

Think of the contrast and comparison of this statement: *"They all seek their own interests."* Not a few. Not some. *All.* Except Timothy. While others chased comfort, applause, or influence, Timothy pursued the interests of Christ.

How do we know if someone is seeking Christ's interests? We will find them caring for people, setting aside their agenda, and investing in others' spiritual growth. We will see compassion in action.

The real test of our priorities is not found in what we say, but in what we seek. Are we running after convenience or Christ's calling? Are we building our platform or His kingdom?

Timothy did not make headlines, but he made disciples. And that is the kind of legacy that lasts.

Jesus, show us where we have been chasing our interests instead of Yours. Redirect our focus. Shape our hearts to seek first Your kingdom, Your people, and Your glory.

DAY 48
Titles Used for Us

*I have thought it necessary to send to you Epaphroditus
my brother and fellow worker and fellow soldier, and your
messenger and minister to my need*
Philippians 2:25

Paul does not just give Epaphroditus a title; he gives him four. Each one tells a story, painting a picture of what it means to live and serve in community.

First, *brother.* The foundation of our identity in Christ is family. We are not just coworkers or acquaintances, we are siblings. We belong to each other.

> *The foundation of our identity in Christ is family.*

Next, *fellow worker.* Epaphroditus was not just spiritually connected; he was *engaged.* Shoulder to shoulder with Paul, laboring for the gospel. Kingdom work is rarely solo work. God calls us to the field together.

Then, *fellow soldier.* There is a battle in this calling: opposition, hardship, fatigue. But there is also camaraderie; fighting side by side, protecting one another, standing firm under pressure.

And finally, *messenger.* Epaphroditus carried more than supplies; he carried encouragement, connection, and hope.

He was the bridge between believers separated by distance, faithfully representing the heart of the Philippians.

Kingdom work is rarely solo work.

Which title speaks to us today? Are we being brothers or sisters to someone who needs care? Are we working faithfully in what God has given us to do? Are we staying strong in the spiritual battle, or carrying a message that lifts someone else's faith?

We each have a part to play. And none of us were meant to do it alone.

Lord, thank You for the people who walk beside us in faith. Help us be brothers, workers, soldiers, and messengers, remaining faithful in every role You have given us. Use our lives to strengthen others.

DAY 49
Quiet Service

I have thought it necessary to send to you Epaphroditus my brother and fellow worker and fellow soldier, and your messenger and minister to my need, for he has been longing for you all and has been distressed because you heard that he was ill. Indeed he was ill, near to death. But God had mercy on him, and not only on him but on me also, lest I should have sorrow upon sorrow.
Philippians 2:25–27

Epaphroditus is not a household name, but he is a hero of the faith. He did not preach to thousands or write letters from prison. He simply showed up. He served. He risked his life to deliver a gift and stand with Paul.

And when he fell ill, deathly ill, his concern was not for himself. He was distressed that the Philippians had heard he was sick. What humility. What self-forgetfulness. Even in weakness, his heart beat for others.

God healed him. Not because he deserved it, but because God is merciful. And Paul saw that mercy was a double gift: for Epaphroditus and himself.

Behind every headline preacher or missionary is someone like Epaphroditus, who is faithful, forgotten by most, but not by God.

Lord, thank You for quiet servants like Epaphroditus. Help us serve faithfully, even if no one notices. Let our lives bring joy to others and glory to You.

DAY 50
Honoring the Humble

I am the more eager to send him, therefore, that you may rejoice at seeing him again, and that I may be less anxious. So receive him in the Lord with all joy, and honor such men, for he nearly died for the work of Christ, risking his life to complete what was lacking in your service to me.
Philippians 2:28–30

Paul commends Epaphroditus and commands the church to honor him. Why? Because he *nearly died* for the sake of the gospel. He laid his comfort, safety, and even his life on the line to serve.

The world celebrates the bold, the famous, the polished. But in God's kingdom, the truly great are those who quietly lay down their lives for others.

We need to recover the holy habit of honoring the humble. The nursery volunteer. The small group leader. The faithful dad. The widow who prays. These are heaven's heroes. We need to notice them. Thank them. Learn from them. And become like them.

Jesus, help us see greatness as You do. Teach us to honor those who serve in quiet, costly ways. And make us the kind of person who would rather be faithful than famous.

DAY 51
Remember This

Finally, my brothers, rejoice in the Lord. To write the same things to you is no trouble to me and is safe for you.
Philippians 3:1

When Paul says, *"Finally, my brothers..."* It is as if he is drawing the people in Philippi close, like a father offering final words to his children. *"If you forget everything else,"* he is saying, *"remember this: rejoice in Him."*

He is sitting in a prison cell, chained to guards, uncertain of the future, and he pens a surprising command: *"Rejoice in the Lord."*

Why? Because circumstances change. The stock market drops. The diagnosis surprises. People disappoint. But the Lord is unchanging. He is the same yesterday, today, and forever. When our joy is anchored to Him, it remains steady through every season.

That phrase, *"Rejoice in the Lord,"* changes everything.

It is not about slapping a smile on tough days or pretending life does not hurt. It is about knowing where to run when it does. When the bottom drops out, joy in the Lord holds us steady. Not because we have less pain, but because we have more of Him.

Joy is not tied to our situation. It is tied to our Savior.

Maybe that is the secret some of us are missing. We are looking for joy in the next vacation, the next promotion, the next big moment. But Paul would say: "Start with Jesus." He is not a part of our joy; He is our joy.

Pause. Breathe deep. Remember, our hope is not in this moment. Our joy is not in this world. Our peace is not up for grabs.

Jesus, remind us that joy is not found in circumstances, but in You. Help us anchor our hearts to who You are, not how we feel. Even when life is hard, help us rejoice in the One who never changes.

Rejoice in the Lord.

DAY 52
Listen Again

Finally, my brothers, rejoice in the Lord. To write the same things to you is no trouble to me and is safe for you.
Philippians 3:1

Some things are worth repeating. Paul knows the Philippians have heard his message before, but he does not apologize for repeating it. Why? Because truth repeated becomes truth remembered. And truth remembered becomes truth lived.

He says, *"It is safe for you."* The Greek word used here carries the idea of being firm, secure, and dependable. Repetition is a safeguard; it protects the mind, grounds the heart, and strengthens the soul. Paul is not being redundant; he is being pastoral.

> *We never stop needing grace. We never stop needing to hear, "Rejoice in the Lord.*

We live in a world of information overload. News headlines, notifications, opinions, and we are flooded with words. But amidst all that noise, we often forget the most important truths: that Jesus is enough, that grace is still amazing, and that the gospel continues to transform lives.

Paul is saying, *"Don't move past what matters most."* We never outgrow the gospel. We never stop needing grace. We never stop needing to hear, *"Rejoice in the Lord."*

Let us be honest. We do not need more new ideas as much as we need deeper roots in the *old* ones. That is where safety is found. In returning to the truth. In rehearsing God's promises. In remembering who we are in Christ.

Father, thank You for repeating what we need to hear. Keep us from becoming numb to familiar truth. Help us listen with fresh ears and a soft heart. Strengthen our faith through the steady rhythm of Your Word.

We never outgrow the gospel.

DAY 53
One Word Resume: Jesus

Finally, my brothers, rejoice in the Lord. To write the same things to you is no trouble to me and is safe for you. Look out for the dogs, look out for the evildoers, look out for those who mutilate the flesh. For we are the circumcision, who worship by the Spirit of God and glory in Christ Jesus and put no confidence in the flesh
Philippians 3:1–3

If anyone had a reason to brag about a spiritual résumé, it was Paul. But here, he proclaims: Do not rejoice in yourself. Rejoice in the Lord.

Why? Because joy does not spring from what we have achieved. Joy flows from who Jesus is and what He has done for us.

Paul warns us to steer clear of the "*résumé builders*." Avoid those who measure their worth by what they do, not who they trust. He calls them "*dogs, evildoers, and mutilators*," descriptors no one expects to read in a letter of encouragement. But Paul is not being dramatic; he is being protective. These were people who said we needed to earn our place with God, that we needed Jesus plus something else (These people were saying that to be genuinely Christian, one must be circumcised).

> *Our value rests securely on what Jesus has done for us, not on what we have done.*

But Paul reminds us of the truth: the people of God are marked not by external rituals, but by inward transformation. We are *"the circumcision."* We are the people who worship by the Spirit, boast only in Christ, and put zero confidence in the flesh.

Where are we finding our worth? Is it in our résumés, our accomplishments, or our goodness? Or in Christ alone?

Our value does not rise or fall based on what we have done. It rests securely in what Jesus has done for us. Rejoice in that. Lean into that. Worship with a heart set free from performance.

Lord, help us to rejoice in You, not in our strength. Strip away our pride and performance-based thinking. Let us glory in Christ alone and worship You through Your Spirit.

> *We are people who worship by the Spirit, boast only in Christ, and put zero confidence in the flesh.*

DAY 54
Not Performance

Finally, my brothers, rejoice in the Lord. To write the same things to you is no trouble to me and is safe for you. Look out for the dogs, look out for the evildoers, look out for those who mutilate the flesh. For we are the circumcision, who worship by the Spirit of God and glory in Christ Jesus and put no confidence in the flesh
Philippians 3:1–3

We live in a world that loves résumés. We dress them up, polish them off, and use them to prove we matter. Even in Christian circles, it is easy to slip into that same mindset. It is difficult to avoid the notion that we must earn spiritual approval through our performance.

But Paul gently grabs our attention and says: *Don't find joy in you. Find it in Jesus.*

His words are strong: "*Watch out for those who tell you that you need to add to Jesus.*" He is referring to individuals who claim that salvation is about Jesus plus something: Jesus plus rules, rituals, or impressive religious efforts.

Jesus + Anything = Not the Gospel

And Paul says *that is not the gospel.*

The real people of God are not those with a perfect spiritual résumé. They are the ones who know they need grace.

People like us who worship by the Spirit, who boast in Jesus, and who have stopped pretending we got it all together.

We do not have to perform to be loved. We do not have to impress God. He already knows us completely and still chose us in Christ. That is why Paul says, *Rejoice in the Lord.* Not in how well we did this week. Not in our failures or successes. Rejoice in Jesus.

Because when we are in Him, our worth is secure.

Jesus, thank You that we do not have to earn what You have already freely given. Teach us to stop measuring ourselves by the world's standards and start rejoicing in Your grace. We want to worship with a free and whole heart because of You.

Jesus + Nothing = More Than Enough

DAY 55
Christ Confidence

Though I myself have reason for confidence in the flesh also. If anyone else thinks he has reason for confidence in the flesh, I have more: circumcised on the eighth day, of the people of Israel, of the tribe of Benjamin, a Hebrew of Hebrews; as to the law, a Pharisee; as to zeal, a persecutor of the church; as to righteousness under the law, blameless.
Philippians 3:4–6

If Paul had a spiritual résumé, it would have been top of the stack.

Born into the right family. Trained under the best. Passionate, disciplined, outwardly righteous. If spiritual success were about credentials, Paul had checked every box. He had religion, reputation, and relentless drive.

But here is what makes Paul's words so powerful: even with all of that, he realized it was not enough.

Are there places in your life where you are still clinging to your version of spiritual success? Maybe you were raised in a Christian home. Maybe you have never missed a Sunday. Perhaps you have volunteered, led Bible studies, or maintained a relatively clean lifestyle.

*The gospel is not about proving ourselves.
It is about receiving Christ*

None of that is bad; it is good. But it is not *Jesus*.

Paul's message is deeply freeing: even the best résumé cannot earn grace. And even the worst one cannot disqualify anyone from it.

In a world where we are constantly being measured, it is easy to slip into striving mode. But the gospel is not about proving ourselves. It is about receiving Christ.

The sooner we let go of self-confidence, the sooner we can rest in Christ-confidence.

Lord, we confess that sometimes we still try to prove ourselves. We chase approval, even with You. Help us release our grip on performance and rest in Your grace. Remind us that knowing You is better than anything we could ever accomplish.

> *The best résumé cannot earn grace. And even the worst one cannot disqualify anyone from it.*

DAY 56
Rubbish, Refuse, Reputation, Recognition, or...

But whatever gain I had, I counted as loss for the sake of Christ. Indeed, I count everything as loss because of the surpassing worth of knowing Christ Jesus my Lord. For his sake I have suffered the loss of all things and count them as rubbish, in order that I may gain Christ
Philippians 3:7–8

There is a moment in every believer's life when the scales tip, when we realize that all our striving, all our status, and all our success are not worth comparing to the treasure we have found in Jesus.

Paul had that moment. He looked at his impressive résumé, his religious accomplishments, his entire identity, and he let it all go. Why? Because knowing Jesus was worth more.

> *All our striving, all our status, and all our success are not worth comparing to the treasure we have found in Jesus.*

He called it rubbish. Trash. In the original language, the word even hints at refuse; that which we throw away without a second thought. That is how radical this trade is.

What is on your "*gain*" list? Is it reputation, comfort, control, achievement, or recognition? None of those are bad in and of themselves. But if they keep us from knowing Jesus more deeply, they are not gains at all. They are losses.

Sometimes following Christ means a quiet sacrifice: saying no to an opportunity, reordering our time, or letting go of a dream. Other times, it means publicly walking away from the world's applause. Either way, it is always worth it.

Knowing Jesus, really knowing Him, is the treasure. Paul is inviting us to make the trade: *everything else for Him.*

Jesus, You are better. Help us believe that today. Open our eyes to see the surpassing worth of knowing You. We let go of anything that competes for our hearts because we want You most of all.

Knowing Jesus, really knowing Him, is the treasure.

DAY 57
He's Enough

*and be found in him, not having a righteousness of
my own that comes from the law, but that which
comes through faith in Christ, the righteousness
from God that depends on faith*
Philippians 3:9

At some point, all of us wrestle with the fear that we are not "*enough*." Not good enough. Not strong enough. Not spiritual enough. We wonder if God could love us when we keep stumbling in the same places.

Paul gets it. He tried to build his righteousness through religious rule-keeping and personal discipline. And if anyone could have succeeded that way, it was Paul. But even he says, "*It doesn't work.*"

What he discovered and what we need to remember is this: righteousness is not achieved; it is received.

> *Righteousness is not achieved; it is received.*

It is not about mustering up good behavior or ticking off the spiritual boxes. It is about being "*found in Christ.*" Covered in His righteousness. Justified, not by performance, but by faith.

That means when God looks at us, He does not see our worst moments or even our best ones. He sees Jesus. That is grace. That is the gospel.

> *When God looks at us, He does not see our worst moments or even our best ones. He sees Jesus.*

That is the kind of love that sets us free, not to do whatever we want, but to walk with joy and confidence, knowing we are fully accepted.

Stop trying to earn what Jesus already gave us. Rest in the righteousness that comes by faith. We are not just tolerated. We are treasured.

Father, thank You that our standing with You does not depend on our perfection, but on Christ's. Help us walk today in the confidence of Your grace, not in the fear of falling short. Let us live like people who have already been made right in Your eyes.

> *We are not just tolerated. We are treasured.*

DAY 58
Power and Suffering

That I may know him and the power of his resurrection, and may share his sufferings, becoming like him in his death, that by any means possible I may attain the resurrection from the dead.
Philippians 3:10–11

There is something beautifully honest about Paul's words. He desires more than information about Jesus. Paul wants to know Him deeply, personally, and experientially. He longs to taste resurrection power, but also to walk with Christ through suffering.

We love the first part: resurrection power. Who wouldn't? Strength, hope, victory, new life. But Paul reminds us that knowing Christ also involves fellowship in suffering. That is the part we would rather skip. Yet suffering is often where we meet Jesus most intimately.

When life falls apart, and we find ourselves clinging to God like never before, something sacred happens. Jesus shows up in the fire, not just after it.

Paul is not chasing pain. He is pursuing Jesus. And if Jesus is in the pain, he wants to meet Him there too.

Intimacy with Jesus changes us. It shapes our character, deepens our hope, and prepares us for the day we see the Lord face to face.

Lord, we want to know You, not just in power, but even in pain. Help us not to run from suffering, but to run to You in the midst of it. Let every season draw us closer to Your heart and shape us for eternity.

DAY 59
Pursuing Him

Not that I have already obtained this or am already perfect, but I press on to make it my own, because Christ Jesus has made me his own.
Philippians 3:12

Paul, the apostle, says, *"I'm not there yet."* He does not pretend he has reached some spiritual summit. Instead, he is still running, still reaching, still learning, all because Jesus reached for him first.

The fuel and motivation for following Christ and remaining committed are rooted in our identity: We press on because we belong.

Jesus made us His own. He took hold of our lives with love, grace, and purpose. Now our job is not to prove ourselves, but to pursue Him with all our hearts.

Maybe today you are tired. Perhaps you feel stuck or unworthy. We do not press on to earn Jesus; we press on because He already claimed us.

Being in Christ and with Christ gives us the strength to keep going, even when we fall. He is not asking for perfection. He is providing direction. Keep pressing on.

Jesus, thank You for making us Your own. We do not run this race alone or unloved. Give us strength to press on today, to pursue You with joy and trust, even when we stumble.

DAY 60
Locked In

*Brothers, I do not consider that I have made it my own.
But one thing I do: forgetting what lies behind and
straining forward to what lies ahead*
Philippians 3:13

We all carry things from the past. Some of it we are proud of. Some of it we wish we could erase. Paul had moments of zeal and moments of shame in his past.

But here is what he says: "*Let it go.*"

Do not live looking backward. Our past does not define our future. Not our mistakes and not our accomplishments. What matters now is where we are headed and Who we are following.

Paul says, "*One thing I do.*" That kind of focus is rare. He is locked in on Christ, stretching every fiber of his being to run toward Him.

It is a beautiful picture: not passive religion, but passionate pursuit. Jesus is ahead of us, calling our name. He is worth chasing.

Do not look back in regret or pride. Let us fix our eyes on what is ahead. And let us run with determination and zeal.

Lord, help us release what is behind: both the guilt that haunts us and the pride that distracts us. Give us fresh focus today to chase after You with all we have got. We want to know You more.

DAY 61
Toward the Goal

I press on toward the goal for the prize of
the upward call of God in Christ Jesus.
Philippians 3:14

There is a prize waiting for us that is better than anything this world could offer.

Paul is not running aimlessly. He is running toward something. Toward Someone. His eyes are on Jesus, the One who called him upward, out of religion and into relationship, out of shame and into grace.

This *"upward call"* is God's invitation to live for what truly lasts. It is not about reaching heaven through our own efforts, but about responding to His love with our lives.

The prize? Christ Himself. The joy of knowing Him fully. The beauty of being in His presence. That is the goal. That is the reward.

When life feels like a long, uphill climb, remember what we are running toward.

Father, give us strength to keep our eyes on the prize. When we get weary or distracted, remind us of what is waiting. Let our hearts be anchored in the joy of knowing You.

DAY 62
In Pursuit

Let those of us who are mature think this way, and if in anything you think otherwise, God will reveal that also to you. Only let us hold true to what we have attained.
Philippians 3:15–16

What does spiritual maturity look like? Paul tells us. Spiritual maturity is a humble pursuit. It is knowing that we have not arrived, yet pressing forward anyway.

The mature believer is not the one who boasts the loudest, but the one who keeps reaching for more of Jesus.

> *Sometimes the most spiritual thing we can do is to keep going. Stay steady. Stay rooted.*

Paul says something important here: "*Don't lose the ground you've already gained.*" In other words, do not drift. Do not let complacency steal what grace has already built in our lives.

Sometimes the most spiritual thing we can do is to keep going. Stay steady. Stay rooted. Do not give up on what God has already shown us.

Lord, grow our maturity, not just in knowledge, but in pursuit. Help us hold onto the truth we have learned and keep walking forward in faith. We want to grow more like Christ every day.

DAY 63
Not Our Forever Home

Brothers, join in imitating me, and keep your eyes on those who walk according to the example you have in us. For many, of whom I have often told you and now tell you even with tears, walk as enemies of the cross of Christ. Their end is destruction, their god is their belly, and they glory in their shame, with minds set on earthly things. But our citizenship is in heaven, and from it we await a Savior, the Lord Jesus Christ, who will transform our lowly body to be like his glorious body, by the power that enables him even to subject all things to himself.
Philippians 3:17–21

The world tries to tell us who we are. It wants us to find our identity in politics, nationality, popularity, success, or some other activity or accomplishment.

But Paul reminds us: *"We are not from here."*

If we belong to Jesus, we are citizens of heaven. That means our values, our goals, and our hope are all rooted in another world; a world where Jesus reigns and will wipe every tear away.

> *Do not get comfortable. This world is not our forever home. Let our hearts stay homesick for heaven.*

Paul contrasts this with people who live as enemies of the cross; those who live for themselves, chase pleasure, and set their minds on earthly things. That road leads to destruction.

But we belong to Christ. And He is coming again. When He does, He will transform our lowly body into something glorious. We will be like Him.

Do not get comfortable. This world is not our forever home. Let our hearts stay homesick for heaven.

Jesus, thank You for making us citizens of heaven. Help us live today with eternity in view. Let our lives reflect Your values, not the world's. We cannot wait to see You face-to-face.

DAY 64
Following Him

Brothers, join in imitating me, and keep your eyes on those who walk according to the example you have in us.
Philippians 3:17

Paul does not say this with pride; he says it with love. *"Watch how I walk. Follow others who walk the same way."* Why? Because faith is lived, not just learned.

We all follow someone: friends, mentors, influencers. The question is: *"Are they leading us closer to Christ?"*

God gives us godly examples to inspire and instruct us. Not perfect people, but faithful ones. People who have made Jesus their goal.

Who are you watching? Who are you imitating?

And even more, what example are we setting? Could someone look at our lives and say, *"That is what following Jesus looks like?"*

Father, thank You for placing godly examples in our lives. Help us to learn from them and grow in faith. And let our lives point others to You through humility, integrity, and joy.

DAY 65
Heartbroken

*For many, of whom I have often told you and now tell you
even with tears, walk as enemies of the cross of Christ.*
Philippians 3:18

This is not a harsh condemnation; it is a heartbroken cry.

Paul is not angry; he is grieving. Some people walk as enemies of the cross, not because they hate Jesus, but because they refuse to live surrendered to Him. They resist the very message that could save them.

And Paul weeps.

When was the last time our hearts broke for someone far from God? It is easy to write people off, to criticize, or distance ourselves. But Paul shows us the way of Christ: weep and pray.

If someone we love is far from God, we cannot give up. We must carry them to the cross. Plead with tears. Love with grace. And trust the One who leaves the ninety-nine to find the one.

Jesus, break our hearts for what breaks Yours. Teach us to love those who resist You with compassion, not condemnation. Help us weep and pray for those who are wandering, because You have not given up on them.

DAY 66
The Quiet Drift

Their end is destruction, their god is their belly, and they glory in their shame, with minds set on earthly things.
Philippians 3:19

Paul describes people ruled by their cravings; their god is their belly. They live for what feels good, not what is true. And the tragedy is, they think it is freedom.

But living for ourselves always leads to destruction.

Being self-focused is not just about blatant rebellion. It is about the quiet drift, when our desires subtly take God's place, when comfort becomes our priority, when pleasure becomes our purpose.

What rules our hearts today? What shapes our decisions and sets our direction?

Freedom comes not from following our appetites, but from surrendering to Christ. Let Him be the center of our thoughts, our joy, and our daily focus.

Lord, reveal anything in us that is taking Your place. We do not want to be ruled by cravings or earthly things. Set our hearts on You. Be the King of our lives and the joy of our souls.

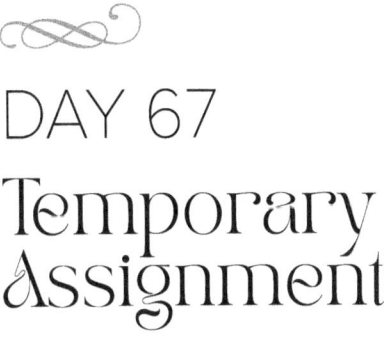

DAY 67
Temporary Assignment

But our citizenship is in heaven, and from it we
await a Savior, the Lord Jesus Christ.
Philippians 3:20

Paul does not say our citizenship will be in heaven someday; he says it is there now. That means our truest identity, our deepest belonging, and our ultimate allegiance are already anchored in eternity. Our names are written in the registry of heaven. We are not tourists here on earth; we are ambassadors, living on temporary assignment until our King calls us home.

But Paul does not just point to where we belong; he points to Whom we are waiting for. We are not waiting for the end of our troubles, for a better economy, or a dream vacation. We are waiting for a Person. Jesus is our Savior, our Deliverer, our Hope. We are not waiting passively, like sitting in a doctor's office flipping through old magazines. Our waiting is active, eager, expectant. We live every day with the awareness that He could return at any moment.

> *Our truest identity, our deepest belonging, and our*
> *ultimate allegiance are already anchored in eternity.*

Waiting well means our priorities shift. We hold the things of earth loosely, knowing they are temporary. We treat others with love, knowing relationships are eternal. We invest in God's work, knowing it will last forever.

The world may try to define us by our job titles, our social status, or our possessions. But heaven knows us as children of the King. And when we live in that reality, it changes how we face today and how we look toward tomorrow.

Lord, thank You that our names are written in heaven and our true home is with You. Teach us to wait eagerly and faithfully, keeping our eyes fixed on Jesus. Let our lives reflect the Kingdom to which we belong.

We are not tourists here on earth; we are ambassadors, living on temporary assignment until our King calls us home.

DAY 68
We Will Be Changed

Who will transform our lowly body to be like his
glorious body, by the power that enables him
even to subject all things to himself.
Philippians 3:21

We live in bodies that ache, break, and slow down. They remind us daily of our limitations, our weakness in sickness, the effects of aging, and the scars of past injury. But Paul reminds us this is not the end of the story. A day is coming when Jesus will transform these frail, mortal bodies into something new, something glorious, just like His own resurrected body. No more pain. No more decay. No more weariness. Only life, strength, and beauty that never fade.

How can we be sure? Because the One who promises transformation has the power to make it happen. The same authority that spoke galaxies into existence, calmed storms with a word, and walked out of the tomb alive is the power that will remake us. Nothing is outside His control. He does not just reign over "*spiritual*" things. Paul says all things are subject to Him. That means our health, our future, our challenges, and our fears are all under His feet.

His promise gives us hope in suffering, courage in weakness, and endurance in the face of trials. We can press on because we know the brokenness we feel now is temporary. Resurrection is coming. Glory is coming. Jesus is coming.

Lord Jesus, thank You for the promise that one day You will make us new. Give us strength to endure our present struggles with hope, knowing You have authority over all things and the power to transform us.

DAY 69
Heaven's Reward

But our citizenship is in heaven, and from it we await a Savior, the Lord Jesus Christ, who will transform our lowly body to be like his glorious body, by the power that enables him even to subject all things to himself.
Philippians 3:20–21

Paul invites us to lift our eyes from the noise of earth to the reality of heaven. Our citizenship is not something we will earn someday; it is already secured. The King has written our names onto the rolls of His Kingdom, and we live here as His ambassadors. Being a citizen of heaven changes everything.

We are not waiting for circumstances to improve or for life to *"finally calm down."* We are waiting for a Person, Jesus Christ, our Savior. And when He comes, He will do more than rescue us from the brokenness of this world. He will transform us completely. These bodies, marked by weakness, pain, and imperfection, will be remade to match His glorious resurrection body. We will be whole, strong, and eternal.

The same power that rules over galaxies, kings, and nations is the power that will restore us.

It is hard to wrap our minds around such a profound transformation. But we can trust it because of the One making the promise. The same power that rules over galaxies, kings, and nations is the power that will restore us. Nothing is beyond His reach; all things are under His authority.

So, we wait, not with dread, but with hope. We live, not for this world's applause, but for heaven's reward. And we trust, not in our strength, but in the power of our Savior who will finish the good work He started in us.

Lord, help us live today as citizens of heaven, waiting eagerly for You. Thank You for the promise that You will make us whole and new. Strengthen our hope, deepen our trust, and keep our eyes fixed on the day we see You face-to-face.

*We live, not for this world's applause,
but for heaven's reward.*

DAY 70
Stand Firm

Therefore, my brothers, whom I love and long for, my joy and crown, stand firm thus in the Lord, my beloved.
Philippians 4:1

Paul is wrapping up his letter, but not before giving us a deep breath of encouragement. We can feel the affection in every phrase: "my brothers," "my joy," "*my beloved.*" This is not cold theology. It is personal. It is heartfelt. And it leads to one simple, powerful command: stand firm in the Lord.

That sounds heroic, like a soldier holding the line. But Paul does not say *"stand firm in your circumstances"* or *"stand firm in your own strength."* He says to **"Stand firm in the Lord."**

That is the secret. When life is shaky, we do not have to be, because He is never shaky.

We stand firm when we anchor our identity in Christ.

We stand firm when we anchor our identity in Christ, not in our past or our performance. We stand firm when our security comes from His promises, not our paycheck. We stand firm when our joy flows from His presence, not our circumstances.

Maybe today it feels like you are barely standing. Doubts, conflict, or discouragement have knocked the wind out of you. Do not try to find strength in yourself. Instead, press into Him. He is steady when everything else is spinning.

> *He is steady when everything else is spinning.*

And just like Paul did for the Philippians, let me remind you: *"You are loved. You are valued. You are not standing alone."*

Jesus, thank You that we do not have to stand firm in our own strength. Help us plant our feet in Your promises. When life gets unsteady, hold us close. Remind us that we will stand as long as we are standing with You.

DAY 71
Unity as Priority

I entreat Euodia and I entreat Syntyche to agree in the Lord. Yes, I ask you also, true companion, help these women, who have labored side by side with me in the gospel together with Clement and the rest of my fellow workers, whose names are in the book of life.
Philippians 4:2–3

Can you imagine hearing your name read aloud in a letter from Paul because you were in conflict with someone in the church? That is precisely what happened to Euodia and Syntyche.

But Paul does not scold them. He pleads with them: "*Agree in the Lord.*" Unity matters deeply to God. Why? Because when we let conflict linger, it stifles joy and strains the body of Christ.

Paul reminds us that resolving conflict is not just the responsibility of the two involved; it is the whole community's calling. He calls on a "*true companion*" to step in and help. That is the role of a peacemaker: someone who reminds us that the gospel is more important than being right.

Maybe today there is a relationship that needs healing. Perhaps it is time to pick up the phone, humble our hearts, and take a step toward peace.

Unity is worth the risk. Because when we live in harmony, we shine with the grace of the gospel.

Lord, give us the courage to pursue peace. If there is someone we need to reconcile with, give us the grace to go first. Help us prioritize unity over being right.

DAY 72
Our Heart Posture

Rejoice in the Lord always; again I will say, rejoice.
Philippians 4:4

Paul says it twice, just in case we missed it the first time: *Rejoice in the Lord always*. Not sometimes. Not when life is easy. *Always.*

This command might feel out of reach, especially when we are walking through hard seasons. But Paul is not telling us to ignore our pain or fake a smile. He is inviting us to anchor our joy in the Lord, not in our circumstances.

Paul is writing from prison, with an uncertain future. Yet his joy is unshakable, because it is rooted in Jesus.

We might not feel joyful today. But joy is not a feeling; it is a posture of the heart. It is a choice to say, *"Even here, even now, I will rejoice in who God is and what He has done."*

When we cannot rejoice in what is around us, rejoice in the One who holds us.

Jesus, You are our joy, our constant in every season. Help us choose to rejoice, even when life is hard. Remind us of all You have done and all You have promised.

DAY 73
Not Our Way

Let your reasonableness be known
to everyone. The Lord is at hand.
Philippians 4:5

"Reasonableness" is a gentle word with a powerful impact. It speaks of kindness, grace, and a willingness to yield, to live in a way that does not demand having our own way.

In a world full of outrage and entitlement, Paul says: Let grace be our reputation. Let gentleness mark our interactions. Be known not for how loudly we speak, but for how lovingly we live.

Why? Because the Lord is near. His presence is close. His return is coming. And His character is worth reflecting on.

Imagine how our homes, friendships, and churches would change if gentleness became the norm. Kindness, care, and respect are the attributes that draw people toward Jesus.

Lord, make us people known for grace. Teach us to be gentle, even when we are frustrated. Let Your nearness shape how we speak, respond, and love others.

DAY 74
Shift Your Focus

Do not be anxious about anything, but in everything by prayer and supplication with thanksgiving let your requests be made known to God.
Philippians 4:6

Anxiety has a way of sneaking in through the cracks. It whispers in the dark, *"What if?"* and piles *"what could be"* on top of *"what already is."* Paul does not dismiss our fears, but he points us to something more substantial: a command anchored in God's character. Do not be anxious.

It almost sounds impossible until we remember who is holding the pen. Paul wrote this from prison. Chains on his wrists, an uncertain future ahead, and yet peace guarded his heart. The difference? He was not chained to anxiety, but to Christ.

When Paul says, *"don't be anxious,"* he is not saying, *"try harder not to worry."* He is saying, *"Shift your focus."* Anxiety thrives when our gaze is on our problems. Peace grows when our eyes are on our Provider.

The same God who fed Elijah with ravens (**1 Kings 17**) and clothed lilies with beauty (**Matthew 6**) can handle what is on our plates. Today, do not let anxiety write the story. Let trust do the talking.

Lord, we confess how easily anxiety takes over. Help us fix our eyes on You, not our fears. Teach us to trust You in every detail of our lives.

DAY 75
Persistent Pestering

Do not be anxious about anything, but in everything by prayer and supplication with thanksgiving let your requests be made known to God.
Philippians 4:6

Supplication is a fancy word for earnest prayer or petition. It is not casual; it is desperate, dependent, and honest. Think of a child tugging on a parent's sleeve. Supplication says, *"God, I need You. I can't do this without You."*

But notice the companion to supplication: thanksgiving. The two walk hand-in-hand. Without thanksgiving, supplication can feel like a list of demands. With thanksgiving, it becomes an act of trust.

When we thank God as we ask, we are remembering what He has already done. Thanksgiving looks back in faith while supplication looks forward in hope. Together, they frame our requests inside God's faithfulness.

The next time we are pleading with God, pause to give thanks. Thank Him for past mercies, even as we cry out for present help. That mixture of petition and gratitude stirs faith in our souls.

Gracious Father, we bring You our needs. But before we ask again, we thank You for all You have already done. Remind us that the same God who carried us yesterday will carry us today.

DAY 76
Everything Means Every "Thing"

Do not be anxious about anything, but in everything by prayer and supplication with thanksgiving let your requests be made known to God.
Philippians 4:6

Notice the word Paul uses *everything*. Not just the big stuff. Not just emergencies. Everything. If it matters to us, it matters to God.

We often treat prayer like a fire alarm: "*Break glass in case of emergency*." But Paul shows us another way. Prayer is a conversation. It is inviting God into the ordinary and the overwhelming. Into the dentist appointment and the diagnosis. Into the daily commute and the crossroads of our future.

Our conversations with God should take place not only when our lives seem to be falling apart, but also when things are going well; we share life along the way. God desires the same for us. He is not distant. He is near. And He delights in hearing our voice. Talk to Him about the ordinary, listen to Him, and remember He loves for us to be in His presence.

Today, bring Him the details. Pray about everything. Do not edit your prayers; offer them as they are. Do not filter them; speak them. The more we pray, the more we realize that peace does not come from controlling life; it comes from surrendering it.

Father, thank You that You care about every detail. We bring our whole day to You; our worries, our hopes, our needs. Teach us to live in conversation with You.

DAY 77
Progression to Peace

Do not be anxious about anything, but in everything by prayer and supplication with thanksgiving let your requests be made known to God.
Philippians 4:6

Life gives us plenty of reasons to worry. Finances. Family. Future. But Paul gives us something stronger than worry: prayer.

When anxiety shows up, God invites us to talk to Him. To lay it all out. To say, *"God, I don't have this, but I know You do."*

Notice the progression: **pray + thank = peace.** Thanksgiving shifts our focus from fear to faith. We remember God's faithfulness, and peace comes rushing in.

Paul says it is a peace that *"surpasses all understanding."* We cannot explain it. We just received it. It is not the absence of problems; it is the presence of God.

So, when worry knocks, answer it with prayer. Again, and again. And watch peace stand guard over our hearts.

Father, we bring You our worries. Thank You that You care, You are near, and You are in control. Fill us with peace that makes no sense, except that it comes from You.

DAY 78
It's Not Sensible

And the peace of God, which surpasses all understanding,
will guard your hearts and your minds in Christ Jesus.
Philippians 4:7

We chase peace in a thousand ways: vacations, distractions, even control. We cannot manufacture the peace Paul describes. Experiencing the peace of God is not a matter of self-help or positive thinking. It is supernatural.

God's peace appears where it does not seem to make sense. Bills may still be due. The diagnosis may not change. The conflict might not be resolved. Yet, inside, we know: "*I am held.*" That is the peace that "*surpasses all understanding.*"

And notice what peace does: it guards. Like a soldier standing watch over our hearts and minds, God's peace pushes back the lies of fear and despair. We do not keep the peace; the peace keeps us.

Where do we need this today? Lay down our worries, lift our prayers, and lean into His presence. The storm may rage, but His peace will stand guard.

Prince of Peace, thank You for guarding our hearts and minds. When we cannot understand, help us rest in You. Surround us with peace that only You can give.

DAY 79
Where Peace Lives

And the peace of God, which surpasses all understanding,
will guard your hearts and your minds in Christ Jesus.
Philippians 4:7

The phrase "*in Christ Jesus*" is more than a closing tag. It is the anchor of the whole verse. God's peace is not found in circumstances, possessions, or even in our best attempts at control; it is found in a Person.

Notice the location of our protection: *in Christ*. Imagine a fortress with walls stronger than stone. Inside, we are safe from the storm, not because the storm disappeared, but because we are shielded by something greater. That is the peace Paul points to. It does not ignore reality; it rests in a greater reality: we belong to Christ.

Think about this: our hearts and minds are guarded, not by our willpower, but by Jesus Himself. His presence is the place where peace lives. His victory is the reason peace holds. His promise is the guard standing at the door of our souls.

When our thoughts spiral or our hearts race, remember where we are: *in Christ Jesus*. That is our address. That is our home. That is where peace reigns.

Lord Jesus, keep our hearts and minds steady, not because we are strong, but because You are our peace. Help us rest today in who You are.

DAY 80
Purposeful Thinking

*Finally, brothers, whatever is true, whatever is honorable,
whatever is just, whatever is pure, whatever is lovely,
whatever is commendable, if there is any excellence, if
there is anything worthy of praise, think about these things.*
Philippians 4:8

Our minds are always working; we are constantly replaying conversations, imagining scenarios, and dwelling on what-ifs. Paul does not tell us to stop thinking; he tells us *what to think about.*

Think about what is true. What is honorable or noble? What is beautiful? What draws us toward Jesus?

This is not about "*positive thinking,*" it is about *intentional thinking*. If we let garbage fill our minds, it will eventually overflow into our actions. But if our thoughts are rooted in Christ's goodness, our heart begins to change, too.

Here is a simple challenge: conduct a thought inventory today. What are you allowing to live in your mind rent-free? What media, conversations, or influences are shaping your inner life?

We do not have to be passive. We can redirect our thoughts to what is life-giving. Fix our minds on what honors God and watch our peace grow.

Lord, teach us to think thoughts that honor You. Help us filter what we read, watch, and dwell on. Fill our minds with truth and beauty that lead us closer to You.

DAY 81
Grounded by Truth

Finally, brothers, whatever is true, whatever is honorable, whatever is just, whatever is pure, whatever is lovely, whatever is commendable, if there is any excellence, if there is anything worthy of praise, think about these things.
Philippians 4:8

We are under constant assault from headlines, half-truths, and internal lies that whisper we are not enough. That is why Paul starts with, "*Think about what is true.*"

Truth anchors us when emotions swirl. Truth grounds us when fear exaggerates. The truth is: we are loved. God is faithful. His grace is enough. Our identity is secure in Christ.

Truth is not just factual; it is foundational. When we focus our minds on what is true, we silence fear and strengthen faith. What are we believing today? We must align our beliefs with God's truth.

Father, help us recognize and reject the lies that creep in. Teach us to dwell on what is true, especially when life feels uncertain.

DAY 82
Attention with Integrity

Finally, brothers, whatever is true, whatever is honorable, whatever is just, whatever is pure, whatever is lovely, whatever is commendable, if there is any excellence, if there is anything worthy of praise, think about these things.
Philippians 4:8

"*Honorable*" is not flashy; it is steady. It is the quiet integrity of a life lived well. Paul invites us to fill our minds with what is worthy of respect, not what is loud or trending.

We become what we behold. So, what if we filled our thoughts with examples of courage, sacrifice, and character? What if we pursued thoughts that lift us up rather than drag us down?

Honor does not demand attention; it inspires it. Let us fix our minds on the noble, not the noisy.

Lord, give us eyes to see what is truly honorable. Shape our hearts to admire and imitate what brings You glory.

DAY 83
A Just Mindset

Finally, brothers, whatever is true, whatever is honorable, whatever is just, whatever is pure, whatever is lovely, whatever is commendable, if there is any excellence, if there is anything worthy of praise, think about these things.
Philippians 4:8

To think about what is just is to align our thoughts with God's justice, His fairness, His righteousness, and His mercy. It is seeing people the way He sees them, not through prejudice or fear.

In a world quick to divide, we are called to think redemptively. When our minds dwell on justice, our lives begin to reflect it; in how we speak, how we treat others, and how we stand up for what is right.

What we meditate on shapes how we live. Justice is not just a cause; it is a mindset.

God, renew our thinking with what is just. Help us reflect Your righteousness in how we perceive others and in our responses to the world around us.

DAY 84
Mental Detox

Finally, brothers, whatever is true, whatever is honorable, whatever is just, whatever is pure, whatever is lovely, whatever is commendable, if there is any excellence, if there is anything worthy of praise, think about these things.
Philippians 4:8

Purity is not just about avoiding impurity; it is about pursuing what is good, clean, and life-giving. Paul is not pushing perfectionism; he is inviting us to protect our hearts from the toxic.

A pure mind sees beauty in God's creation, joy in truth, and peace in surrender. Purity does not feed on envy, bitterness, or lust. It looks for the holy in the ordinary.

What we let linger in our thoughts eventually shows up in our lives. We must intentionally choose thoughts that refresh our souls and honor God.

Lord, purify our thoughts. Help us filter out what pollutes and focus on what gives life. Make our hearts a place where Your peace can dwell.

DAY 85
Our Gaze Redirected

Finally, brothers, whatever is true, whatever is honorable, whatever is just, whatever is pure, whatever is lovely, whatever is commendable, if there is any excellence, if there is anything worthy of praise, think about these things.
Philippians 4:8

"*Lovely*" is more than pretty. *Lovely* reflects God's beauty and grace in a broken world. It is the quiet strength of kindness, the soft light of peace, the unexpected joy in a hard moment.

Paul knew life was not always lovely, but he also knew that beauty could be found even in suffering. When we fix our thoughts on what is lovely, we train our hearts to see hope.

There is more good around us than we sometimes notice. Look for it. Dwell on it. Let the lovely redirect our gaze toward heaven.

Father, open our eyes to see the beauty You have woven into our lives. Help us focus on what is lovely, even when life feels heavy.

DAY 86
Proud to Repeat

Finally, brothers, whatever is true, whatever is honorable, whatever is just, whatever is pure, whatever is lovely, whatever is commendable, if there is any excellence, if there is anything worthy of praise, think about these things.
Philippians 4:8

Commendable means worth talking about, in the best way. Not gossip or criticism, but praise. Things that lift others. Acts of grace. Stories of redemption.

Paul reminds us: We do not have to amplify the worst parts of life. We can choose to highlight what is good, praiseworthy, and life-giving. That is what healthy minds do.

Today, think about something we would be proud to repeat and then make it a reality or share it with others.

Jesus, help us speak and think about what brings You joy. Let our minds dwell on what is worthy of praise, not what pulls others down.

DAY 87
Not Passive but Purposeful

Finally, brothers, whatever is true, whatever is honorable, whatever is just, whatever is pure, whatever is lovely, whatever is commendable, if there is any excellence, if there is anything worthy of praise, think about these things.
Philippians 4:8

Excellence does not mean flawlessness. It means whole-heartedness; doing things in a way that honors God and blesses others. Thinking on excellence means noticing effort, growth, beauty, and diligence.

When our minds focus on excellence, we become people who build up instead of tearing down. We start seeing potential instead of problems. We lean into doing our best for God's glory.

Excellence begins in the mind before it manifests in our lives.

God, train our thoughts to pursue what is excellent, not for applause, but for Your name's sake. Let us live with purpose, not passivity.

DAY 88
Tuned to Praise

Finally, brothers, whatever is true, whatever is honorable, whatever is just, whatever is pure, whatever is lovely, whatever is commendable, if there is any excellence, if there is anything worthy of praise, think about these things.
Philippians 4:8

Paul ends with a sweeping invitation: "*If there's anything praiseworthy*, anything at all, dwell on it.

This is the mindset of gratitude. Of noticing God's fingerprints in the small and the sacred. It is tuning our hearts to praise, even when life is not perfect.

We will always find what we are looking for. If we look for the good, the gracious, the God-honoring, we will see it. And it will change the way we live.

Lord, help us be people of praise. Shift our focus from what is wrong to what is worthy. Let our thoughts give You glory.

DAY 89
Stretched Through Obedience

What you have learned and received and heard and seen in me—practice these things, and the God of peace will be with you.
Philippians 4:9

Learning is not the hard part; it is the practicing that stretches us.

Paul encourages the Philippians to take everything they have seen and heard in him: his joy, his endurance, his love, and *live it out*. Because following Jesus is not just about information; it is about transformation.

The promise is beautiful: "*The God of peace will be with you.*" That means peace does not just come from knowing the right things; it comes from living them out.

What is one truth you have been learning lately? Put it into action today. Take that next step. Obedience always opens the door to deeper peace.

Father, we do not want to just learn about You; we want to live like Jesus. Help us take what we have received and walk it out in real time. Fill our lives with the peace that comes from obedience.

DAY 90
Revived Concern

I rejoiced in the Lord greatly that now at length you have revived your concern for me. You were indeed concerned for me, but you had no opportunity.
Philippians 4:10

Paul rejoiced, not just because his needs were met, but because their love for him came alive again.

It is easy to underestimate the impact of simple encouragement. A text, a meal, a gift, a prayer. These small acts revive concern, and they refresh weary hearts.

When we show up for someone, we are showing them the love of Christ. And our concern might be the very thing that stirs joy back into their life.

Who needs your encouragement today? Ask God to place someone on your heart and then follow through.

Because in God's economy, concern is never wasted. It brings joy, healing, and spiritual strength to those who receive it.

Lord, thank You for the people who have revived our hearts through their kindness. Show us how to do the same for others. Help us be a source of joy and encouragement today.

DAY 91
Unshakable Contentment

Not that I am speaking of being in need, for I have learned in whatever situation I am to be content. I know how to be brought low, and I know how to abound. In any and every circumstance, I have learned the secret of facing plenty and hunger, abundance and need.
Philippians 4:11-12

Paul found something most of us spend a lifetime chasing: contentment.

He did not find it on a beach, in a promotion, or through comfort. He learned it in hunger and hardship, in plenty and poverty.

The secret? Contentment does not come from what we have, but from *Who we have*. When Christ is enough, *everything else becomes enough, too.*

This does not mean we will not have desires. It means they will not define us.

If you have been waiting for a specific outcome to feel joy again, let Paul's words encourage you: *You can learn contentment right where you are.*

Jesus, we confess how often we look to people or things to make us happy. Teach us the secret Paul learned about being content in You alone. Let our hearts rest in Your sufficiency today.

DAY 92
Learned Peace

Not that I am speaking of being in need, for I have learned in whatever situation I am to be content. I know how to be brought low, and I know how to abound. In any and every circumstance, I have learned the secret of facing plenty and hunger, abundance and need.
Philippians 4:11-12

Paul does not sugarcoat life. He knew what it was to be hungry, to be beaten, to be abandoned, to wonder where the next provision would come from. Yet he does not complain. He says he learned how to be brought low. That word "learned" is essential; it was not natural, it was not instant. Contentment in times of need was something God had to teach him, one moment at a time.

We often think that peace comes when a problem is solved, but Paul reminds us that Christ is enough, even in the midst of struggle. When we are low, He lifts us. When we are empty, He fills us. When we are needy, He shows Himself faithful.

Sometimes God allows seasons of lack so that we discover His sufficiency more deeply. Our need becomes the classroom where we learn the lesson of trust.

Jesus, when we feel low and our needs overwhelm us, remind us that You are all we need. Teach us the lessons of trust and dependence so that we may find peace, not in what we lack, but in who You are.

DAY 93
Rooted in Contentment

Not that I am speaking of being in need, for I have learned in whatever situation I am to be content. I know how to be brought low, and I know how to abound. In any and every circumstance, I have learned the secret of facing plenty and hunger, abundance and need.
Philippians 4:11-12

We often think that contentment is hardest in seasons of need, but abundance brings its own challenges. When life is full, and blessings overflow, it is tempting to forget the Giver and place our joy in the gifts. Paul says he had to learn contentment even in abundance. Why? Abundance can lead to pride, greed, or a false sense of security.

Abundance is meant to turn our hearts toward gratitude, not self-sufficiency. God gives so that we may give. He blesses us so that we may bless others. Abundance becomes dangerous only when it causes us to forget that Christ remains our source.

Paul's contentment did not rise and fall with his bank account. Whether he had much or little, his joy was anchored in Christ. And when Christ is our treasure, abundance becomes an opportunity for worship, not a distraction from it.

Lord, thank You for seasons of abundance. Guard our hearts from pride or false security. Help us hold loosely to the blessings You give and use them to honor You and bless others. Keep us rooted in contentment that comes from Christ alone.

DAY 94

Tapping into Divine Strength

I can do all things through him who strengthens me.
Philippians 4:13

This verse is a favorite on coffee mugs and locker room walls, but it is often misunderstood.

Paul is not saying, "I can accomplish anything I dream up." He is saying, "I can endure anything life throws at me, *because Christ gives me strength.*"

In hunger, He strengthens me. In abundance, He steadies me. In sorrow, He sustains me. In weakness, He carries me.

We do not have to muster our own grit to get through today. We have access to divine strength. Not to conquer the world, but to remain faithful in whatever season we are in.

When we feel tired or overwhelmed, remember: Christ does not expect us to be strong enough. He promises to be strong for us.

Lord, we cannot do this on our own, and we do not have to. Thank You for being our strength. Carry us through today, moment by moment. We trust You to give us what I need.

DAY 95
Him Working in and Through

I can do all things through him who strengthens me.
Philippians 4:13

Paul does not say, "I can do all things because I'm tough" or "I can do all things if I just push harder." His confidence is rooted in two simple words: *"through Him."*

That little phrase changes everything. It reminds us that the source of strength is not within us but flows through us. Like a branch abiding in the vine, our ability to endure, to love, to persevere does not originate in our own reserves. It comes from Christ's life at work in us.

"Through Him" means dependence, not independence. It means resting in His grace when our own strength runs dry. It means drawing from His wisdom when ours is clouded. It means surrender, acknowledging that we are not the source of life but rather its recipients.

Instead of waking up each day thinking, I *have to do this*, we can wake up praying, *Lord, do this through me.* When Christ is the channel, ordinary people become instruments of extraordinary grace.

Jesus, teach us to rely on You as our source. Help us stop trying to muscle through life on our own and instead let Your strength flow through us today.

DAY 96
Continual Strengthening

I can do all things through him who strengthens me.
Philippians 4:13

Notice the verb *strengthens*. Christ is not passive. He is not distant. He is actively at work fortifying His people. Paul does not just say Christ gave him strength once; he says Christ *strengthens* him in the present tense, indicating an ongoing, continual process.

Think of a coach in the middle of a race, shouting encouragement and giving water to the runner. Think of a spotter in the gym, lifting the bar when an athlete's arms give out. Christ does not watch from the sidelines; He comes alongside and infuses His strength into our weakness.

That is why Paul could face prison chains, hunger, and hardship with contentment. He was not banking on his own grit. He was banking on Christ's presence. The same is true for us. Whatever weight we carry, Christ is not asking us to lift it alone. He is promising to strengthen us, moment by moment, as we depend on Him.

Lord, thank You that You are strengthening us even now. Remind us that we are never alone in our struggles. Give us the courage to face today, knowing that Your strength is greater than our weakness.

DAY 97
Ministry of Presence

Yet it was kind of you to share my trouble.
Philippians 4:14

Sometimes the greatest gift we can give someone is not a solution; it is presence. The Philippians did not remove Paul's trouble, but they *shared it*. And Paul called that kindness.

When someone is hurting, our compassion reminds them they are not alone. That is part of what it means to be the body of Christ: we carry each other's burdens.

God did not design us to go through life solo. He meant for us to link arms and walk together through both the joy and the pain.

Who in your life needs you to come alongside them today, not to fix them, but to *be with them*?

Father, make us aware of the burdens others carry. Help us offer kindness, not just solutions. Teach us how to show up with presence, empathy, and love.

DAY 98
A Legacy of Generosity

And you Philippians yourselves know that in the beginning of the gospel, when I left Macedonia, no church entered into partnership with me in giving and receiving, except you only. Even in Thessalonica you sent me help for my needs once and again.
Philippians 4:15–16

The Philippians were a church that not only talked about support but also practiced it. They gave consistently and sacrificially, even when other churches did not.

And Paul remembered it.

Generosity is never forgotten in God's kingdom. Every dollar, every meal, every moment you give in Jesus' name plants eternal seeds.

We may not always see the fruit, but heaven does; our quiet acts of support echo in eternity.

What if we stopped seeing generosity as a duty and started seeing it as a legacy? A way to leave behind a trail of lives lifted, burdens lightened, and gospel work sustained?

Lord, thank You for the example of the Philippians. Make us generous like them; faithful in giving, joyful in partnering, and committed to seeing others thrive in Christ.

DAY 99
Investing in Eternity

*Not that I seek the gift, but I seek the fruit that increases
to your credit. I have received full payment, and more.
I am well supplied, having received from Epaphroditus
the gifts you sent, a fragrant offering, a sacrifice
acceptable and pleasing to God.*
Philippians 4:17–18

Paul wants the Philippians to know something important:
their generosity is not about his need, but about *their own
growth and development.*

Yes, Paul is thankful for their support. But what really ex-
cites him is the spiritual fruit that their giving produces. Their
generosity is like an investment in eternity. Every gift, every
sacrifice, every act of service is building a harvest in their
lives.

God sees it. He counts it. And He multiplies it.

When we give to gospel work, not just financially, but with
time, encouragement, and prayer, it matters more than we
think. It brings joy to others, honor to God, and growth to
your own heart.

Today, do not underestimate the impact of our kindness
and faithfulness. Heaven is keeping track, and the fruit is
growing.

Lord, help us to be cheerful givers; not just of money, but of time, words, and presence. Thank You that every act of generosity bears fruit in Your kingdom. Use what we give to make much of You.

DAY 100
Faithful Provider'

And my God will supply every need of yours
according to his riches in glory in Christ Jesus.
Philippians 4:19

This promise is often quoted, but it is essential not to over-look its context. Paul is speaking to generous believers who have prioritized God's kingdom. And now he assures them: *God's got you.*

He does not promise extravagance. He promises *enough.* Not always what we want, but always what we need.

And notice the source: not our bank accounts, our employers, or our hustle, but *"God's riches in glory in Christ Jesus."* That is an endless supply.

When we give, we are not losing. We are trusting. And God delights in taking care of givers who reflect His heart.

When we are tempted to hold back out of fear, remember: our Provider is faithful. Always.

Father, thank You for supplying what we need. Help us trust You more, give freely, and live with open hands. You are generous, and we want to reflect Your heart.

DAY 101
Still Writing the Story of Glory

To our God and Father be glory forever and ever. Amen.
Philippians 4:20

Paul ends his letter the way he lived his life: giving glory to God.

No matter the need, the gift, the hardship, or the miracle, Paul traces it all back to one Source. *"To our God be glory."*

That is the heartbeat of the Christian life: not just to make it through, but to reflect the goodness of the One who walks with us.

When we pause to give God glory, it re-centers our souls. It reminds us that He is still on the throne, still worthy, still writing the story.

Let this be our exhale today. Whatever has happened, joy or sorrow, progress or setback, end your day the way Paul ended his letter: *To God be the glory.*

God, You deserve all the glory. In the good and the hard, in the quiet and the loud, we praise You. Let our lives be a reflection of Your goodness and grace.

DAY 102
Prepared for the Day

Greet every saint in Christ Jesus.
The brothers who are with me greet you.
Philippians 4:21

We can be tempted to skip over verses like this one, just closing remarks, right?

But notice what Paul says: "*Greet every saint.*" Not just the leaders. Not just the ones who are easy to love. *Every saint.*

That means every person in our church family is valued and matters. God cherishes each one. Each one deserves encouragement, attention, and dignity.

The gospel is not just vertical, between God and us; it is horizontal, too. It binds us together in a family where no one is overlooked.

Take a moment today to notice someone you usually pass by. Offer a warm word, a smile, a genuine greeting. You may be the voice of grace they needed.

Jesus, help us see people the way You do. Give us eyes to notice and hearts to welcome every saint in Christ. Let love flow freely in our church family.

DAY 103
Quiet Victories

All the saints greet you,
especially those of Caesar's household.
Philippians 4:22

Did you catch that? *Even Caesar's household* had saints in it.

In the unlikeliest place, at the heart of the Roman Empire, in the palace of a pagan emperor, God was at work. People were coming to Christ.

Paul is celebrating a quiet victory. A reminder that no place is too dark, no system too broken, no person too unreachable for the gospel.

Perhaps there is someone in our lives who appears distant from God. Or we are in a setting where faith feels out of place. Take heart, Jesus plants light in the darkest corners.

His grace is working in places we do not even know.

Lord, thank You that Your gospel cannot be stopped. Bring light into the darkest places in our communities, workplaces, and families. Let us be part of your quiet victories.

DAY 104
Daily Peace

The grace of the Lord Jesus Christ be with your spirit.
Philippians 4:23

Paul ends where he began, with *grace*.

Not just for their circumstances, but for their *spirit*. For their inner world. For the part of them that fights fear, wrestles doubt, and needs daily peace.

We may not know what tomorrow holds, but we *do* have this: *"The grace of the Lord Jesus Christ, with us."*

It is grace to sustain, to strengthen, to settle our souls.

So, wherever we are, whether celebrating, struggling, or simply showing up, this is our promise: His grace is enough. For every day. For every moment. For us.

Jesus, we receive Your grace today. Let it fill every weary part of us. Strengthen our spirits and remind us that we are never alone. Your grace is our peace.

DAY 105

Living a Father-Filtered Faith

"Rejoice in the Lord always; again I will say, rejoice...
The grace of the Lord Jesus Christ be with your spirit."
Philippians 4:4, 23

Thank you for walking through Paul's letter to the Philippians with me. Paul's epistle is a thank-you note, a missionary update, a theological treasure chest, and a joyful pep talk, all rolled into four short chapters. He wrote it from prison, yet it pulses with gratitude and joy. He had every reason to complain, but instead, he worshiped.

Paul reminds us that joy is not anchored in circumstances, but in Christ. "*To live is Christ*" (**1:21**) is more than a catchy motto; it is a way of life. Whether Paul was chained to a guard, pleading with two feuding friends to reconcile, or dreaming about the resurrection to come, his eyes stayed fixed on Jesus.

And that is the invitation for us:

- **Keep Christ at the center.** Our story begins and ends with Him. Make Him the reference point when life feels chaotic.

- **Live as citizens of heaven.** Our identity is secure. We are not defined by yesterday's mistakes or today's headlines; Christ's victory defines us.

- **Press on toward the goal.** Do not get stuck in regret or distracted by comfort. There is a race to run, a crown to win, and a Savior worth pursuing.

- **Stand firm together.** The church is not a collection of spiritual lone rangers; it is a family. When one suffers, all suffer. When one rejoices, all rejoice.

And finally, Paul leaves us with a promise: *"My God will supply every need of yours according to his riches in glory in Christ Jesus"* (**4:19**). That is not just a promise for food and shelter; it is a promise that He will give us the strength, courage, and grace to live this letter out.

Jesus, thank You for speaking through this letter, for reminding us to rejoice, to press on, and to stand firm in You. Teach us to keep our eyes on You when life is hard and to celebrate Your goodness in every season. Strengthen us to live as citizens of heaven, to love our brothers and sisters well, and to pursue You with all our hearts

A Father-Filtered Faith Anchored in Christ

He who calls you is faithful; He will surely do it.
1 Thessalonians 5:24

When I look back over this journey through Philippians, I am struck again by how practical and personal Paul's words are. He was not writing abstract theology from a marble desk or crafting slogans for church walls. He was chained to a Roman guard, waiting on a verdict, and yet his heart was overflowing with joy. Every word of this letter beats with a steady rhythm of trust, a faith filtered through the Father's hand and anchored in the unshakable person of Jesus Christ.

A Father-filtered faith begins where control ends. It is forged in spaces where our plans fall apart, and our prayers feel unanswered. It is a faith that believes God wastes nothing, not the waiting, not the tears, not the unanswered questions. It sees life through a different lens, one shaped by the conviction that our Father is always good, always present, and always purposeful.

Paul's story reminds us that faith does not remove chains; it redeems them. The same God who opened Lydia's heart by the river and shook the prison at midnight was shaping Paul's heart through confinement. And that is the beauty of a Father-filtered life: even when we cannot trace His hand, we can trust His heart.

When Paul wrote, *"He who began a good work in you will bring it to completion,"* he was not offering motivational fluff. He was declaring the confidence of a man who had seen God's faithfulness up close. The work of grace does not stop when the storm begins. It deepens. It refines. It roots us more deeply in Christ until we can say with Paul, *"For to me to live is Christ, and to die is gain."*

A Father-filtered faith does not mean life will be easy. It means life will be anchored; anchored in the presence of Christ when circumstances shift, anchored in the peace of God when anxiety rises, anchored in the joy of the Lord when disappointment knocks, and anchored in the strength of the Spirit when obedience costs us something precious.

The Philippian believers knew this. They were a small church in a proud Roman colony, surrounded by power, politics, and paganism. Yet Paul calls them his *"joy and crown."* Why? Because their faith endured. They did not just believe in Christ; they belonged to Him. Their joy was not a mood but a mindset. Their unity was not uniformity but humility. They had learned, as we must, that true joy is not found in the absence of problems but in the presence of Christ.

A Father-filtered faith looks for God's hand in the detours. It sings at midnight. It chooses humility over pride, service over status, contentment over comparison. It lives worthy of the gospel by remembering that citizenship in heaven changes how we walk on earth.

Walking through these verses and chapters, we have traced Paul's journey from prison cell to praise, from suffering to song, from anxiety to peace. But this is not merely Paul's story; it is ours. God is still writing His faithfulness into the pages of our lives. We are each a work in progress. And every day, the Father filters what reaches us, allowing only what can grow us, shape us, and draw us closer to His Son.

Faith like that is not passive. It listens. It leans in. It looks up. It keeps showing up when it is easier to quit. It continues to believe that the same God who began the story is strong enough to finish it beautifully.

There will be days when the noise of life tries to drown out His whisper. On those days, remember what Paul discovered: joy is not the absence of noise; it is the presence of Jesus. When feeling restless, rejoice. When feeling anxious, pray. When feeling overlooked, serve. When feeling weak, lean hard into grace. For underneath it all is the Father's hand, steady, sure, and strong.

We may never see how many lives our faith touches. Paul did not. He simply wrote letters, prayed from prison, and trusted God with the results. Centuries later, we are still reading those words, still finding strength in his surrender, still learning that peace and purpose are found not by striving, but by resting in Christ.

The book of Philippians ends with a simple benediction: *"The grace of the Lord Jesus Christ be with your spirit."* Grace; that is where it starts and where it ends. Every step of this journey has been grace: grace that saves, grace that sustains, grace that strengthens and secures.

A Father-filtered faith keeps coming back to that grace again and again, knowing that every breath, every burden, and every blessing passes through His loving hands before it ever reaches ours.

As you close this book, pause and give thanks.

Thank Him for the closed doors that became new directions.

Thank Him for the hardships that shaped your heart.

Thank Him for the people who walked beside you, prayed for you, and reminded you of His truth.

And above all, thank Him for Jesus, the anchor of our souls, the joy of our salvation, and the faithful finisher of every good work.

Your Father sees you. He loves you.
He is not finished with you.
So stand firm. Rejoice in the Lord always.
Keep your eyes on Christ, your heart open to His Word,
and submit your life to His will.
Because when faith is filtered through the Father, fear
loses its grip, grace grows stronger, and joy becomes
unshakable.

May your faith be anchored in Christ.
May your days be filled with gratitude.
May your heart find peace in His presence.
And may your life, like Paul's, become a living letter of grace;
A testimony that says to the watching world:
"The Lord is near, and He is enough."

APPENDIX A
Understanding the Joy-Filled Letter of the Philippians

From the echo of Roman chains comes one of the most uplifting books in the Bible. The Apostle Paul, writing from a prison cell around A.D. 60–62, crafted a letter filled not with bitterness or despair, but with radiant joy and deep confidence in Christ. Philippians is not a treatise on theology or a theological debate; it is a window into a heart that beats with gratitude and gospel hope even when surrounded by suffering.

Modern readers may find it strange that one of the most joy-filled books in Scripture was written behind bars. But that is the paradox of the Christian life: joy is not the absence of struggle but the presence of Jesus in the midst of it. In Philippians, Paul teaches us that when Christ becomes the center of our lives, our circumstances no longer define our peace; He does.

The Background: A Church Born in Adversity

Philippi was a proud Roman colony in Macedonia, settled largely by retired soldiers who were fiercely loyal to Caesar. Citizenship there carried honor and privilege, and to proclaim, "*Jesus is Lord*" was to challenge the empire's creed that "*Caesar is Lord*." When Paul and Silas first brought the gospel to Philippi (**Acts 16**), they met Lydia, a wealthy merchant who opened her home to them. A demon-possessed slave girl was freed, and a Roman jailer was saved after an earthquake shook his prison. From this unlikely beginning, a diverse church, united in Christ by a blend of races, classes, and stories, was born.

Now, years later, Paul writes to that same community from a Roman prison, expressing gratitude for their partnership in the gospel and encouraging them to remain steadfast in the face of persecution. The Philippians had sent one of their own, Epaphroditus, to deliver a gift to Paul. He nearly died serving him, which made the letter both deeply personal and profoundly pastoral.

The Purpose: Joy, Unity, and the Mind of Christ

Paul's tone in Philippians is unlike any other letter. He is not addressing doctrinal confusion or moral failure; he is calling believers to maturity; to live as *"citizens of heaven"* (**Phil. 3:20**) in a world that celebrates power, pride, and self.

At the heart of the letter lies a poetic confession known as the Christ Hymn (**Phil. 2:5–11**), which captures the entire gospel story in miniature. In it, Paul reveals both the nature of Christ and the pattern for the Christian life:

- Christ humbled Himself: choosing servanthood over status.

- Christ obeyed unto death: choosing the cross over comfort.

- God exalted Him, revealing that true glory comes through humility.

Paul uses this hymn as the center of gravity for the entire book. Every command, example, and exhortation circles back to this truth: To know Christ is to become like Him.

The Themes That Shape Philippians

- Joy in Suffering: Joy that comes not from what happens to us, but from who holds us.

- Humility and Unity: A shared life modeled after Christ's servanthood.

- Christ as the Pattern of Life: The believer's story is meant to mirror Jesus' story.

- Resurrection Hope and Heavenly Citizenship: We live in the present with the values of the world to come.

- Generosity and Contentment: True wealth is found in dependence on "*the One who strengthens*" (**Phil. 4:13**).

Paul's Message in Motion

Throughout the letter, Paul gives flesh and blood examples of what it looks like to live the "*Jesus-shaped*" life. In himself, Paul shows that chains cannot bind the gospel (**1:12–26**). In Christ, he shows that true greatness comes through humility (**2:5–11**). In Timothy and Epaphroditus, he points to faithfulness expressed in selfless service (**2:19–30**). In his own past and future, he models letting go of worldly status to gain Christ (**3:4–14**). And in the Philippian community, he teaches contentment and peace in the face of anxiety (**4:4–13**).

The Relevance: Why Philippians Still Speaks Today

We live in a world of comparison, consumption, and constant noise. The joy of Philippians cuts through that noise with a clear reminder: our worth is not found in our résumé, our possessions, or our performance; it is found in our Redeemer.

When Paul says, "*To live is Christ, and to die is gain*" (**Phil. 1:21**), he is not speaking from theory; he is speaking from transformation. He invites us to a joy that suffering cannot erase and a peace that circumstances cannot undo. In every age, Philippians calls believers to anchor their identity in Jesus; the source of all contentment, unity, and hope.

Outline of Philippians

I. **Greeting and Thanksgiving (1:1–11)**
   Paul greets the saints and expresses joy for their partnership in the gospel. His prayer centers on love, discernment, and maturity.

II. **The Gospel in Chains (1:12–26)**
   Paul's imprisonment advances the gospel; his life and death both serve Christ.

III. **Living Worthy of the Gospel (1:27–2:18)**
   Call to unity, humility, and courage; includes the Christ Hymn as the model for believers.

IV. **Living Examples of Christlikeness (2:19–30)**
   Timothy and Epaphroditus exemplify selfless service.

V. **Counting All as Loss for Christ (3:1–4:1)**
   Paul contrasts religious pride with knowing Christ personally and calls believers to press on.

VI. **Standing Firm in Peace and Contentment (4:2–9)**
   Urges reconciliation, rejoicing, and the peace of God that surpasses understanding.

VII. **Gratitude and Final Blessing (4:10–23)**
   Paul thanks the Philippians for their generosity and reveals the secret of contentment.

Conclusion: The Secret of Joy

If Paul could find joy in a cell, perhaps joy is not found in getting free, but in knowing Who sits beside us. Philippians reminds us that the gospel does not just change our destination; it changes our disposition. It calls us to live as people who radiate hope because our hearts are anchored to the unshakeable love of Christ.

As we reflect on the devotionals that we read or as we re-read them, let us not rush past Paul's words. Let them sink deep. Let them shape how we think, speak, and live. For when we live like Christ, we begin to experience what Paul discovered in the darkness: the joy of the Lord is not situational; it is supernatural.

Thanks for reading. If you enjoyed this book, please consider leaving an honest review.

Available on Amazon.com

If you are interested in receiving free daily devotionals, visit atthetablewithhim.com

www.ingramcontent.com/pod-product-compliance
Lightning Source LLC
Chambersburg PA
CBHW060419130626
46555CB00005B/2134